A DAY IN THE LIFE OF A MINIMALIST
ESSAYS AND ARGUMENTS

JOSHUA FIELDS MILLBURN

Asymmetrical Press
Missoula, Montana
www.Asymmetrical.co

Published by Asymmetrical Press.

You probably won't read this sentence.

Library of Congress Cataloging-in-Publication Data
A day in the life of a minimalist / Millburn — 3rd ed.
Print ISBN: 978-1-938793-06-6
eISBN: 978-1-938793-07-3
WC: 34,299
1. Title. 2. Happiness. 3. Minimalism. 4. Simplicity. 5. Self-improvement.

Cover photo by Adam Dressler
Cover design by Dave LaTulippe

Author info:
Fiction: joshuafieldsmillburn.com
Essays: theminimalists.com
Email: themins@themins.com
Twitter: @JFM

ASYM METR ICAL

For Colleen

The truth will set you free.
But not until it is finished with you.

—David Foster Wallace

a day in the life of a minimalist
essays and arguments

PART ONE

HELLO

Foreword
by Colin Wright

I'll tell you this now: Joshua Fields Millburn can write.

That's one of the first things I learned about him back in 2010 when we met at a coffee shop not far from Strand Books in New York City. He was generously bringing me a phone to replace one I'd managed to lose while traveling, and we decided to meet up in person, both finding ourselves in Manhattan the same week.

He told me, "I'm kind of a writer. I mean, I like to write." He also said, "I'm thinking of changing my lifestyle. Going more minimal." He continued, "Any ideas on how best to move forward?"

I told him to start a website and begin writing online.

Josh is a generous guy, bringing phones to strangers in New York, but that's not why the world of minimalism—perhaps even practical philosophy as a whole—is better off. It's better off because from day one of launching *The Minimalists* he wanted to improve his own life while helping others do the same. And he wanted to do it well.

A handful of months after we met in that New York coffee shop, I received an email from Josh telling me he'd worked out a plan of attack for the web with his buddy Ryan Nicodemus—a chap he'd been chatting with about life, and with whom he'd discovered a close philosophical kinship. He said that he'd managed to scrap most of his excess possessions, and was diving headfirst into a minimalist lifestyle. He was enjoying every moment of it.

This is where Josh's actions backed up his words. Not just in terms of doing what he said he wanted to do, but about his being a writer. In a blogging ecosystem where most people were producing tired, trite, demographic-focused platitude-posts, he was writing essays. And the difference between what was being done and what he was doing didn't end with the moniker.

Instead of aiming for the tempting, fluffy mass at the center of the lettered-population-parabola, Josh wrote for people who wanted to read well-conceived, purposefully delivered thoughts. Instead of copping out with hackneyed "Top 37" lists or curating collections of stale advice from non-experts around the Internet, he took his time thinking, writing, editing, and publishing. More than most people I can think of, he's really imbued that last word with the reverence it has historically possessed. *Publishing.*

This collection of essays is the result of years of thought and careful wording, edited and organized and published in an eminently digestible format so the good ideas contained within can continue breathing life into the people they touch and the lives they change along the way.

I've enjoyed the hell out of keeping up with Josh's work and personal development these past couple of years. I hope you do, too.

Colin Wright is an author, entrepreneur, minimalist, and full-time traveler who moves to a new country every four months based on the votes of his readers. He is the author of nine books; a twice-monthly premium newsletter, Exiles; a blog, Exile Lifestyle; and is the cofounder of Asymmetrical Press, a community and publishing house for writers and creative types. Discover more about Colin at ExileLifestyle.com.

A Kind of Brief Opening Statement of Sorts
by Joshua Fields Millburn

In the beginning I was lost. But I made it look like I knew the way.

I've noticed that a lot of people search for happiness in the strangest ways—often through things or ephemeral indulgences that, by definition, don't last. I know I did. I was discontented with much of my life. I was unhappy, unfulfilled, dissatisfied. That's incredibly difficult to confess publicly, but it's true.

People used to tell me that I had "everything figured out." I had the six-figure salary, the huge house, the luxury cars (yes, *cars*, plural), and all the material possessions that were supposed to bring me happiness. But I was not happy; I was not content or satisfied with my life. So, like many Americans, I tried to buy happiness, searching the malls and the stores for that next thing that would satiate my thirst. But those purchases didn't make me happy, at least not for long.

Sure, I experienced that cocaine-like high at the cash register, but by the time my credit card statement arrived, I was overwhelmed with discontent and anxiety and stress. To mask my depression, I bought more stuff, thinking maybe this or that would finally make me happy. It never did. Another month, another credit card statement. I was earning great money, but I was spending even better money, and that equation never works in your favor (unless you're the credit card company).

I reached a point in my late twenties where I was experiencing so much discontent that something had to change. But what? I wasn't sure. I was in debt. I was unhealthy and out of shape and I felt like crap. My relationships were in shambles because I didn't treat the people closest to me like they mattered. I was working 70–80 hours a week at a job I didn't enjoy, leaving little time for me to pursue my passions. I wasn't growing as an individual; in fact, I felt as if I was dying inside. And I certainly wasn't contributing beyond myself. It got to the point where I didn't know what was important anymore.

And then, at age 28, a series of life-changing events unfolded in front of me. In the fall of 2009, my mother died of cancer. Less than a month later, my six-year marriage ended abruptly. I stood frozen for a while, staring at the mess around me, and when I thawed, I started questioning everything in my life, from my job and my professional future to my health and my personal relationships. Around the same time, I stumbled across this seemingly radical concept called minimalism, a movement I slowly embraced, shedding the majority of my material possessions over the next year, discovering what was actually important in my life (hint: it wasn't the stuff I owned). I showed my best friend of twenty years, Ryan Nicodemus, how I had simplified my life and, more important, how I was discovering happiness not through my possessions but through experiences and relationships and contribution. Because he was in a similarly discontented situation, he too began simplifying his life, shedding excess stuff, finding meaning in the non-material world.

Ryan and I started a website, *TheMinimalists.com*, in December 2010 with two objectives in mind: to document our journey into minimalism and to inspire others to take a similar excursion. We did not, however, expect the rapid growth we soon experienced. It turned out that our message of *living a meaningful life with less stuff* resonated with a lot of people, people who were willing to share our message with their friends and family and coworkers. In less than a year, we were fortunate enough to witness the start of a small movement as our online audience grew organically to more than 100,000 monthly readers and we were featured in dozens of television, radio, print, and online media outlets, including the *Wall Street Journal*, CBS, NPR, CBC Radio, FOX, and NBC. Moreover, our essays were featured on scores of popular websites, including *Zen Habits*, *Time* magazine's #1 blog in the world.

Our website documents in great detail our journey into minimalism and our continuous growth through experimentation. Our first full-length nonfiction book, *Minimalism: Live a Meaningful Life*, chronicled our troubled pasts, our accidental discovery of minimalism, and the entire new world of happiness, contentment, and purpose we experienced after incorporating minimalism into our daily lives.

In 2011, we left our corporate jobs to focus full-time on our passions. Since then we have published three books about minimalism, written hundreds of essays about simple living, and embarked on a 33-city whirlwind tour across the United States and Canada, meeting many of our incredible readers, exchanging ideas and listening to their heartfelt stories of radical change. I've also been able to focus on my passion—writing literary fiction—and have published two fiction books, *Falling While Sitting Down* and *Days After the Crash*, with a finished novel, *As a Decade Fades*, on the way. All five of our published books, including my fiction, went on to become bestsellers, allowing us to get our message into the hands and minds of people in 151 countries around the world.

While Ryan and I both write essays for our website, often collaboratively, this book is a "best of" collection of my own personal writings about minimalism and simple living. This book contains 50 of my most important essays—some short, some long—from 2011 and 2012. These essays have been edited and often rethought and rewritten to accord with the motif of this collection. They are purposefully organized into nine sections—*lifestyle*, *goals*, *experiments*, *clutter*, *relationships*, *changes*, *philosophy*, *consumer culture*, and *work*—covering a variety of topics, viewpoints, and arguments within those themes. The order herein is deliberate; this collection is meant to be read in sequence from beginning to end. Doing so will result in an experience that is different from reading the essays individually throughout the web, connecting various concepts that might otherwise seem unconnected. You will notice some repetition throughout these chapters. This repetition is intentional; it reinforces my core values and beliefs, repeatedly hammering home what I consider to be the most important aspect of living a purpose-filled, meaningful life. These essays were written to encourage you to think critically about the excess in your life, to help you discover what is most important to you, and, ultimately, to inspire you to take action towards living more intentionally.

As a special thank you to my readers, I included two never-before published essays in this collection: "What If Everyone Was a Minimalist?" and "Work-Life Balance," as well as the previous foreword from my good friend Colin Wright.

Whether you obtained this book from your local library, ordered it online, purchased it at your local independent bookstore, or a friend gave you a copy, I hope you enjoy it. If you do, I'd appreciate your help in spreading the message: please share this book with a friend, sign up for free essays at our website, and leave a helpful review on Amazon if you have a moment. I sincerely hope this book adds value to your life.

JFM

31 Somewhat Brief, Somewhat Banal Personal Things You May or May Not Know About Me

Each year time betrays me, and I get one year older. This year is no exception. Last year, as the sun set on my roller-coaster twenties, I turned 30 and shared "30 Life Lessons I've Learned" on our website. It's been a year since then, and today (June 29, 2012) is my 31st birthday.

I am inherently suspicious of lists, as they're often vapid and overdone and, honestly, not very well written (e.g., *6 Ways to Get Six-Pack Abs in Six Days!*, *11 Bloggers Reveal 11 Surefire Hacks to Create a Successful Life-Hacking Blog*, etc.). Furthermore, I don't enjoy wedging trivial details about my personal life into essays unless those details serve the greater good. But alas, in an effort to get to know each other, here's my attempt at a list. Perhaps there's beauty beneath the banality. Perhaps not.

31 Things You May or May Not Know About Me

1. I believe the meaning of life is *growth* and *contribution*. If

whatever I'm doing doesn't serve one—or both—of these values, then it's a waste of time. Each year I grow; the more I grow, the more I have to give.

2. Yes, Joshua Fields Millburn is my real name, not a pen name. *Fields* was my father's middle name, too. I generally introduce myself as *Joshua*, but a bunch of people call me *Josh*. Fine by me. Seriously, I want you to feel comfortable, so call me whatever you want—Joshua, Josh, Millie, JFM—just don't call me collect.

3. I was born in Dayton, Ohio, in 1981 (year included for people as mathematically challenged as I am).

4. I'm 6'2", 165-ish lbs. (though I used to weigh 230–240 lbs. at my corpulent zenith).

5. I've never lived anywhere but Ohio. (Update: as you'll discover towards the end of this book, I moved to a mountainside cabin in Montana in October 2012.)

6. I don't desire to be a nomad or a peripatetic writer, but I've traveled more in the last year than all 30 previous years combined: I embarked on an amazing 33-city meetup tour and spoke at several events.

7. I grew up in a fairly dysfunctional household (before it was cool to be dysfunctional).

8. The title story in my short story collection, *Falling While*

Sitting Down, is based on my tumultuous childhood and is about 90% autobiographical.

9. I graduated high school half a year early to attend audio engineering school (way back in the 90's when we still recorded on reel-to-reel tape), where I learned to record everything from bluegrass and jazz to death metal and hip-hop.

10. I moved out on my own on my 18th birthday and got a sales job once I discovered that I couldn't make much money as a recording studio engineer.

11. Although I grew up Catholic, I'm not particularly religious. If anything, I'd say I'm open to religion. One of my closest friends—Adam Dressler, the guy who takes most of the photos for our website—is a Harvard-educated pastor. Other friends are atheists. For me, religion is abstract and abstruse. All I know is that I don't know it all.

12. I don't have a college degree.

13. When I was 22 I started taking a few college classes at night in hopes of one day—sometime in the distant future—becoming an English teacher. But then the corporate ladder got in the way.

14. Now it *is* the distant future, and with my online writing class, I'm the only teacher I know without a degree.

15. I wasted my 20's climbing the corporate ladder, working 70–80 hours a week, 362 days per year, attaining "impressive" titles like store manager and regional manager and director of operations, none of which made me feel fulfilled.

16. Instead of fully pursuing my dream at 22, I bought a too-big house and a luxury car and started racking up debt.

17. It took getting "everything I ever wanted" to realize I didn't want everything I ever wanted.

18. I eventually led a large group of people—as many as 100 employees in 16 locations—where I learned that I enjoy helping people grow.

19. Over the years, I've interviewed well over 1,000 people, hired over 200, and fired/laid-off nearly 100, the latter of which never gets easier with time. I'm glad I don't have to do that anymore.

20. I was married to a wonderful woman for more than six years, though we grew in different directions and eventually parted ways shortly after my mother died in 2009. We're still close; relationships can change over time.

21. I didn't start reading books until I was 21. Once I discovered literary fiction, I was hooked. I didn't know how, but I knew I wanted to be a part of it.

22. I didn't start writing until I was 22.

23. I wasn't serious about writing until I was 28. Sure, I had a couple failed attempts at writing a novel, but I didn't seriously pursue writing until a few years ago.

24. I have an inch-thick stack of discouraging rejection letters from agents and publishers from my 20's.

25. Since receiving those letters, I've published five #1 bestselling books. Hell, I might collect all those letters one day and publish them as a book. I could call it *Dear Author: Rejection Letters to a Bestselling Writer.*

26. I left my corporate job a few months before I turned 30 so I could pursue my dream. When I left the corporate world, I didn't expect our audience to grow as much as it did. But I'm incredibly thankful it did, and I'm thankful you read my words. Your support means the world to me. Thank you for giving me a purpose.

27. When I started our website 18 months ago, I didn't know what a *blog* was. (Seriously!) But I needed an outlet to share my writing and my experiences with other people. So I asked my best friend, Ryan Nicodemus, if he'd be willing to share his experiences—and *my* experiences—with the world. He said yes, and soon we created *The Minimalists*, started publishing essays, which we soon realized were called *blog posts*. We stuck with calling them *essays*, though, because we believed it better categorized what we were writing. The

word *essay* derives from the French infinitive *essayer*, "to try" or "to attempt," and we were writing about the changes we were attempting to make in our lives.

28. I've known Ryan (the other half of *The Minimalists*), since we were fat little fifth graders, brothers from another mother.

29. I currently own one pair of blue jeans.

30. I learned how utterly uninteresting I am while writing this list.

31. I don't dance, I just pull up my pants and lean back.

PART TWO

LIFESTYLE

What If Everyone Was a Minimalist?
An Unpublished Essay

Not long ago, a newspaper reporter asked me a common question: "The world wouldn't work if everyone was a Minimalist, would it?"

"Yes it would," I answered. "And it did—for thousands of years."

In evolutionary terms, it wasn't until very, very recently that we began accumulating material possessions, treating our *wants* as *needs*, manufacturing newer, bigger, more ostentatious *wants* along the way, until what once seemed like a mental illness to many cultures became acceptable and, eventually, the norm, allowing us to not only accept the mass-collecting of stuff into our lives, but to *expect* it, to expect to accumulate things in an effort to (somehow) be happy, content from accumulation, fulfilled by our stuff, which, as George Carlin put it, is like taping sandwiches to your body in an effort to satisfy your hunger.

But wouldn't the economy crash if everyone became a minimalist? That's the common follow-up question, and the answer is a little more complicated than a simple yes or no. I would argue that our economy is already broken. This isn't hard to see when you step out from among the trees and peer at the forest from a distance. The problem is that we're attempting to fix the problem with the problem. That is, we're attempting to "stimulate" an economy that's already overstimulated, which seems tantamount to giving a pornography-addicted man more pornography to keep him from dealing with the real problem.

Yes, everyone *could* be a minimalist and the world would go on. A few hundred years ago, nearly everyone *was* a minimalist by default. People weren't living simply, they were simply living. Since then, we've evolved technologically, medically, and even intellectually; but one could argue that we would evolve even quicker if everyone was a minimalist (i.e., if everyone cleared the clutter from their lives and focused on what was truly important). Sure, we would live differently if everyone adopted this lifestyle, and many of the things we're used to—strip malls, billboards, Walmart, &c.— might not be as prevalent as they are today. But is that a bad thing?

Moreover, I'm not too concerned with such hypothetical questions, as they are vastly unrealistic. Rather, I'm concerned with the people who are interested in living happier lives, people who want to live more intentionally, people who are willing to question the possessions in their life in search of deeper meaning. Those are the people whom I want to hear the message of simple living. Maybe that's not 100% of the population, but it's enough to make a significant difference in the world.

I Was Not a Minimalist, Until I Was

I am not an expert. I just play one on the Internet.

Or rather, I wasn't an expert on anything—until I was.

You see, at 18 I didn't know how to be a leader. But then I took an entry-level sales job, spent a decade working my way up the corporate ladder, and eventually led a group of 100 people in 16 locations. Over time, I slowly became an expert at leading people.

At 22 I didn't know how to run a successful business. But then, with no formal education, I learned. In the course of time, I opened 14 profitable retail stores for a large corporation, managed a $52 million operating budget, and eventually oversaw the operations for 150 retail stores (which I now realize, as a minimalist, is rather ironic in retrospect). Over time, I slowly became an expert at business.

At 25 I didn't know how to get in shape or lose the excess weight that plagued me. But then I changed my diet, began a simple exercise routine, and lost 70 pounds. And now people regularly rely on me for diet and exercise advice. Over time, I slowly became an expert at health.

At 27 I didn't know how to live a meaningful life. But then I confronted my discontent, spent two years paying off immense personal debt, and started looking for happiness in more important areas: health, relationships, growth, and contribution—not material possessions. Over time, I slowly became an expert on intentional living.

At 28 I didn't know how to be a minimalist. My three-bedroom home was filled with superfluous possessions to prove it. But then I started questioning my stuff, removing one by one the unnecessary things from my life, eventually jettisoning 90% of my material possessions, replacing them with worthwhile experiences. Over time, I slowly became an expert on minimalism.

At 29 I didn't know what a blog was. (Seriously!) But then I needed an outlet to share my writing and my experiences with other people. So I asked my best friend, Ryan, if he'd be willing to build a website and share his experiences—and *my* experiences—with the world. He said yes, so we created *The Minimalists*, started publishing essays (which we later realized were called "blog posts"), and grew our readership to tens-of-thousands of people in 150 countries. Over time, we slowly became experts at blogging.

Approaching age 30, I didn't think it was possible to leave my corporate job to pursue my dream of writing literary fiction. But then I discovered it was. I had already simplified my life, paid off my debt, changed my spending habits, and radically reduced my cost of living. So I sold my house, paid off my car, eliminated nearly all my bills, and moved into a tiny $500-per-month minimalist apartment. And then I quit. Over time, I slowly became an expert at leaving the corporate world in the pursuit of dreams.

At 30 I wasn't a published author. I had a stack of

rejection letters from agents and publishers to prove it. But now, at 31, I have published three #1 bestselling books on my own and co-founded my own publishing community—Asymmetrical Press—where we help writers and other creative types circumvent the old guard. Over time, I slowly became an expert in the publishing world.

Last year I didn't think I could be a teacher, since I don't have a college degree. But then I learned I could use my training experience from the corporate world, combined with my love and passion and obsession with writing, to add value to people's lives. Thus, I started an online writing class this spring. When the class quickly filled up, I was shocked; so I offered a summer session. And when that class reached its capacity, I offered a fall session. Most importantly, my students—ranging from teenagers to Ph.D.'s—have found tremendous value, have grown as writers, and have given me the opportunity to contribute to their successes. Over time, I slowly became an expert at writing and teaching.

I didn't tell you any of this to brag or boast or inform you of how great I am. I am not great—far from it. There won't be a life-size bronze statue of Joshua Fields Millburn occupying the streets of Dayton, Ohio, anytime soon. I am flawed and tattered and perfectly imperfect—just like you.

I wasn't able to do any of the above because I was smarter or better or funnier or more toothsome than the next guy. Instead, there were two commonalities among all these paths to expertise: time and action.

None of it happened overnight; it took time. And it wasn't easy; it took consistent action—incremental actions that morphed into habits over time. Now, when I look in life's rearview mirror, everything is different. Over time, I slowly became an expert. And so can you.

I Don't Need Much

When life is simple, I don't need much to live.

I don't need much to pursue my passion. A cup of coffee, a place to write, and my thoughts tumbling onto the page will do just fine.

I don't need much to cultivate meaningful relationships. A pretty girl, a full-belly sunset, and a good conversation sound just right to me.

I don't need much to live a healthy life. Daily exercise, healthy foods, and plenty of breathing while walking keeps me living healthily.

I don't need much to contribute to others. A day at a soup kitchen, an afternoon with Habitat for Humanity, and some advice for a friend in need goes a long way.

I don't need much to grow as an individual. Daily action, small incremental changes, and a commitment to constantly improve my life will keep me growing.

I don't need much to live a meaningful life.

And neither do you.

A Day in the Life of a Minimalist

I do not have a daily routine. I no longer need one.

I do, however, have habits on which I focus every day.

Don't get me wrong, I used to have a daily routine—before I quit my six-figure job to pursue my passions and live a more meaningful life. And I hated that routine. Every day felt like *Groundhog Day*: awake to a blaring alarm, shower, shave, put on a suit and tie, spend an hour or more in mind-numbing traffic, succumb to the daily trappings of emails and phone calls and instant messages and meetings, drive home through even more mind-numbing traffic, eat something from a box in the freezer, search for escape within the glowing box in the living room, brush my teeth, set the alarm clock, sleep for five or six hours, start all over again in the morning. That was life most days. The same thing over and over and over. Wash. Rinse. Repeat.

And then last year I decided it wasn't for me anymore. I realized working 60–80 hours a week to make the money to buy more superfluous stuff didn't fill the void I felt inside. It only brought more debt and anxiety and fear and loneliness and guilt and stress and paranoia and depression. So I canceled my routine. Or, rather, I traded in my routine for better habits.

It didn't happen overnight, but over a few years I pared down my possessions, got into the best shape of my life, paid off my debt, jettisoned my TV, eliminated Internet at home, left corporate America, started pursuing my passions, stopped buying junk, and started living a more meaningful life—a life focused on growth and contribution.

During that time of personal growth I developed new habits I love, habits I look forward to each day, habits that make me happy: exercise, writing, reading, establishing new connections with people, and building upon existing relationships.

I also developed the habit of *contribution*. Giving is living—we don't feel truly alive unless we contribute to other people in meaningful ways. Donating time to Habitat for Humanity, local soup kitchens, and various other community organizations has been a starting point on my journey towards developing this habit. And I enjoy contributing to the readers at our website and inspiring them to change their lives.

Many readers ask me what my typical day looks like now that I'm no longer forced into an unnecessary routine. My answer is always the same: every day is a blank page, although there are habits I act upon daily.

Presenting last Thursday as an example, this is how I enjoyed the day...

I woke at 4:50 a.m. without an alarm, excited and refreshed. These days my habit is to wake when my body tells me it's rested. But there is no routine.

I ate a banana, drank a cup of coffee, and then wrote from 5 a.m. to 11 a.m. As I primarily write literary fiction, I prefer writing in the morning when it's quiet and I'm closest to the dream world. My writing room contains only a desk, a chair, a laptop, and my notes—the only things I need. Nothing else. There's no phone, no Internet, no clock—no distractions. Just me and my habit, which I enjoy immensely. Each day I write until I don't feel like writing anymore. But there is no routine.

After a writing-fueled morning (interrupted only by push-ups every hour or so), I walked to the neighborhood park and alternated between pull-ups and push-ups under the midday sun. Exercise is important for me, and I enjoy it daily. But there is no routine.

I showered, dressed (jeans and a teeshirt), and walked to a local burrito joint to eat a modest, vegetarian lunch. I eat when my body tells me I'm hungry, irrespective of the time (I don't own a watch). Some days I eat lunch at noon; other days I might eat at 10 a.m. or 3 p.m. But there is no routine.

After my meal, I walked to my favorite coffee shop, ordered an herbal tea, used their Internet connection to check my email and publish some writing online, and then visited with some of the regulars (as well as a few strangers). There were 37 emails in my inbox, which was okay as I only check email two or three times a week. Sometimes more, sometimes less. But there is no routine.

After a couple hours on the Internet, I walked to a park, sat on a bench, and read a novel. Some days this habit invites me to devour chapter after chapter, hour after hour; other days I read for only half an hour. But there is no routine.

After a few chapters, I hit the gym with my best friend (and online writing pal), Ryan Nicodemus, and enjoyed some cardio and weight training. We habitually visit the gym four or five days a week. We drop by at different times each day. But there is no routine.

Throughout the day I made sure I was hydrated. Besides coffee and herbal tea, I drank only water. No alcohol. No sugary drinks. No soda (or 'pop,' for those of us in the Midwest). I attempt to drink my body weight in ounces of water each day, which isn't always easy—so sometimes I drink only half that. But that's okay: there is no routine.

I own a car, but I didn't drive it on Thursday. I didn't need to. It was a nice day, so I walked instead (even though Dayton, Ohio, isn't exactly the most walkable city in the world). Some days I need to drive to where I want to go; other days I can walk. But there is no routine.

Later that evening I enjoyed dinner and a conversation with a friend, and afterwards we walked to a local concert. Other days I might watch a movie at the indie theater or visit a friend's house or spend time in an art gallery or volunteer a few hours of my time, all habits I enjoy. But there is no routine.

After the concert, I walked a few miles by myself, gathering my thoughts. It had been a beautiful day, followed by a beautiful night—a denim sky illuminated by a waning crescent moon, a million diamonds afire, and the prospect of a new day at midnight.

The good news is my life is no different than yours, minus the routine. Sure, the details are different, the circumstances are different, but we all have the same 24 hours in a day. We all have one life to live, and that life is passing by one day at a time. The only real difference lies within the decisions we make and the actions we take.

A Minimalist's Thoughts on Money

I'm dizzy from the shopping mall
I searched joy, but I bought it all
It doesn't help the hunger pains
and a thirst I'd have to drown first to ever satiate.

—John Mayer,
"Something's Missing"

I don't think about money the same way I used to.

I used to think money was more important than just about everything else in my life. So I sacrificed to make money, and then I sacrificed more to make more money, and then I sacrificed even more to make even more money, working too many hours, forsaking my health, forsaking the people closest to me, forsaking everything important in pursuit of the almighty dollar.

The more things I forsook, the more important the money became. Something was missing.

I made good money—great money—during my days in the corporate arena, but the problem was that I spent even better money. And that was a serious source of dissatisfaction in my life, one that would haunt me for most of my twenties.

When I was 19, I worked six or seven days a week, and I earned more than $50k a year, which for a degree-less poor kid from Dayton, Ohio, that's a lot of money—more money than my mother ever earned. The problem was that when I was earning $50k, I was spending $65k; and then when I was earning $65k, I was spending $80k. Eventually, I'd worked my way up the corporate ladder, working 362 days a year (literally), and I was earning a six-figure salary. That sounds great, but I was spending more than I was bringing home, and that equation never balances.

So instead of bringing home a great salary, I brought home debt and anxiety and overwhelming amounts of discontent. My love and hatred of money (love of spending it, hatred of never having enough) was, in fact, my largest source of discontent.

Call me stupid. Go ahead, you should. I *was* stupid. But I wasn't stupid just because I was wasting my income. No, I was far more stupid because of the value I gave to money. I told myself I was a number; there was a dollar sign on my head; I could be bought. I told others they could take my time and my freedom in exchange for green pieces of paper with dead slave owners' faces printed on them.

But that changed when I stopped giving such importance to money. Sure, I need money to pay rent, to put food on the table and gas in the car, to pay for health insurance. But I needn't struggle to earn money to buy crap I don't need anymore.

Minimalism has allowed me to get rid of life's excess so I

can focus on what's essential. And now, at 31, I make far less money than my stupid 19-year-old self, and yet I'm not in debt, I'm not struggling, and most important, I'm happy.

Now, before I spend money, I ask myself one question: *Is this worth my freedom?*

For example: Is this coffee worth $2 of my freedom? Is this shirt worth $30 of my freedom? Is this car worth $30,000 of my freedom?

In other words, am I going to get more value from the thing I'm about to purchase, or am I going to get more value from my freedom?

Don't you think it's a question worth asking yourself?

These days, I know that every dollar I spend adds immense value to my life. There is a roof over my head at night, the books or the music I purchase add unspeakable value to my days, the few clothes I own keep me warm, the experiences I share with others at a movie or a concert add value to my life and theirs, and a cup of tea with my best friend becomes far more meaningful than a trip to the mall ever could.

I no longer waste my money, and thus it's far less important to pursue it endlessly.

First Thing in the Morning

I like to wake up early. Often as early as 3:30 a.m., before the rest of the world. Not every day, but often.

I don't have an alarm clock. I follow my body's cues. I typically go to bed by 9 or 10 p.m., but life happens and sometimes I go to bed later. Some nights I sleep three hours, some nights nine. I wake when my body tells me it's rested. As soon as I'm awake, no matter the time, I get out of bed immediately and start my day. Getting out of bed—that's the secret.

For the longest time I didn't know why I enjoyed waking up so early. Even when I worked in the corporate world, I didn't know why I liked the mornings. I just knew that my days went better when I did. In fact, during my twelve years in corporate America, one of the few things that gave me solace was my early morning time in solitude.

After reflecting on it for a while, I discovered three reasons why I enjoy my early mornings. While there is no routine, my mornings typically involve three activities I'm excited to do, three things that make me feel productive, three things I enjoy immensely, three things that add value and give meaning to my life. I didn't realize this until recently.

First thing in the morning, as soon as I wake, I do one or more of the following:

Read. I love to read literary fiction. For me, literary fiction, unlike any other art form, has the ability to show us what it means to be a human being in incredibly complex times. Thus, I read to better understand my own life.

Write. Writing is my passion. I write fiction to convey the feelings and emotions that can only be told through the lives and consciousness of characters within a narrative. I write nonfiction (e.g., the essays you're currently reading, as well as long-form narrative nonfiction) to add value to other people's lives.

Exercise. My health is incredibly important to me. Plus, exercising first thing in the morning—even if it's for just 18 minutes—starts the day out right.

Whenever I do any of these activities in the morning, the rest of my day tends to flow more freely.

Do you have anything you're excited to get out of bed and do?

A Minimalist's Thoughts on Diet

I no longer catch the common cold. Yes, that's right: I don't get sick anymore. Ever. I didn't get sick even after hugging 2,000 people during our 33-city meetup tour, many of who were themselves sick and didn't want to hug me for fear of "getting me sick." I hugged them anyway, because I don't believe in "catching the common cold." I no longer maintain the environment for the common cold to live in my body.

So you don't ever get sick, Joshua?

Nope.

Never?

No, not at all.

I bet that's a strange thing to read, right? I know that it's a strange thing to write. And I know that it might sound like complete nonsense, but I'd like you to bracket your skepticism for a moment and hear me out.

It's been two years since my last cold. Clearly, much has changed over the last two years: I started *The Minimalists* with Nicodemus, I left the corporate world, I started pursuing my dream, I wrote the best literary fiction of my life, I published several bestselling books, I cofounded a community for writers and creative people, and I started teaching an online writing class.

There is, however, one subtle change I haven't talked about much: my gradually changing diet. A few years ago, I used to be a meat-'n'-potatoes kind of guy. And I used to catch a cold several times a year; even when I wasn't sick, I didn't feel great. To be honest, I felt like crap most of the time. I used to weigh 70 pounds more than I weigh now, I had stomach problems, and I was tired and sluggish and I lacked the energy necessary to live an active, fulfilling life.

Today, my diet is markedly different, and I've never felt more alive. I no longer have issues with energy or focus like I used to. And most important, I feel better. My stomach problems are gone, the excess weight is gone, I no longer get sick, and the spring is back in my step. And this is why…

Food. My diet today consists mostly of plants and unprocessed foods. I eat an abundance of vegetables and fruits. I'm particularly fond of avocados, spinach, broccoli, and anything green—not because they taste good, but because these foods makes me *feel* outstanding. I also consume beans and/or rice at most meals, and I eat fish and nuts several times a week. My ideal meal looks something like this: a bowl containing a small portion of rice, half an avocado, a diced tomato, a piece of grilled salmon, a handful of almonds, and a massive spinach-carrot-cucumber side salad with almond oil and lemon.

Avoid. There are quite a few foods I've drastically reduced— or completely eliminated—from my diet: bread, pasta, sugar, gluten, meat (other than fish), bottom-feeding seafood (lobster, crab, and other garbagemen of the sea), most dairy products, and anything processed or packaged. There are many so-called experts out there—I am *not* one of them—but it was my friend Common Sense who advised me to avoid most of these foods. Think about it: besides humans, do you know of any animals who drink another mammal's breast milk? What other animal eats bread or pasta or candy bars? Our bodies are not meant to consume this junk (one can make a good argument for eating meat, but I know that I feel much better without it, and *feeling better* is my true test). *But Joshua, how do you get enough protein, calcium, iron?* Well, how does the world's strongest primate, the gorilla, consume enough of these nutrients? Gorillas eat vegetables and fruit—leaves and bananas (many green vegetables are comprised of 20–45% protein). And you likely need less protein than you think.

Intermittent Fasting. I eat two meals a day (generally no snacks besides liquids), both consumed within an eight-hour window, usually around 11 a.m. and 6:30 p.m. I fast during the day's remaining 16-hours (i.e., 7 p.m. to 11 a.m.), consuming only water, herbal tea, or black coffee during those times. This is much easier than you think. If you want to lose weight, particularly fat, then intermittent fasting will make a drastic difference in your life. And yes, this means I skip breakfast. Visit Martin Berkhan's website to find out why and to read more about I.F.

Water, Liquids, and Juice. I drink roughly half my bodyweight in ounces of water each day. I weight 165-ish pounds (I used to weigh 240 pounds), so I drink 80–90 ounces of water per day. I'm also fond of drinking 1–2 powdered green drinks every day for increased vitality (I enjoy Amazing Grass GREENSuperFood). Additionally, I own a masticating juicer that's great for juicing fresh vegetables and fruits, directly supplying my body with the nutrients I need. I also drink coffee, albeit appreciably less than I used to, as well as herbal tea and almond milk, but I eliminated cola and all sugary liquids from my diet (including fruit juices, which contain shockingly high amounts of sugar).

Supplements. Although I eat a large quantity of nutrient-rich foods, I find it important to take daily supplements with each meal: multivitamin (comprehensive nutritional health), vitamin B-complex (cardiovascular health), fish oil (omega-3 fatty acids for heart health), St. John's Wort (mood health), and cranberry supplement (urinary tract health). I noticed a considerable difference in my body after two months of these daily supplements.

Exercise. I exercise every day, but I don't spend a ton of time or effort or focus on it. Instead, I do only two things: 1) I walk three-to-eight miles a day, allowing me plenty of time to think and breathe and de-stress as I meander the streets of Dayton, Ohio, and 2) I workout for 18 minutes. I'm not worried about building vanity muscles; I'm concerned with how I feel. I've discovered that when I eat and exercise in ways that help me feel good, lean muscles are a nice bonus. You don't have to kill yourself to become fit. My friend Vic Magary is the fittest guy I know and he exercises 10 minutes a day. Same goes for my friend Maria, who records videos of her quick around-the-house workouts. Everyone has 10–20 minutes a day to dedicate to their health, right?

Sleep. Because of diet and exercise, I need less sleep than I used to. Most mornings I awake around 3:30 a.m., after five or six hours of sleep. Some days, however, I sleep later, until 7 a.m. or 8 a.m. I let my body dictate how much sleep I need, which happens to be far less sleep than just a couple years ago.

Stress. You don't *get* stressed, you *do* stressed. If I were to ask you what a stressed person looks like, you'd easily be able to mimic his or her physiology. That's because when we start to feel stressed, we do certain things with our bodies: frowning, shallow breathing, muscle tensing, etc. Once you become aware of your stressed physiological state, you can change your physiology—the way you move your body—to become unstressed. Sure, nearly everyone feels stressed these days, but I am significantly less stressed than I've ever been, because I make an effort to be aware of my triggers and change my physical movements accordingly. When I feel overwhelmed, I'll change my breathing pattern, I'll take a walk, I'll exercise, I'll look in the mirror with a big grin, or I'll make sure no one's looking and I'll jump up and down like a crazy person—anything to get me out of that stressed state. (N.B. these techniques also effectively combat depression, anger, and sadness, too.)

Most important, after changing my diet and embracing a healthier lifestyle, I feel amazing.

But Joshua, your diet sounds so boring and unentertaining! I don't think so, but then again I no longer look at food as entertainment. Food is fuel, nothing more. I can still enjoy a great conversation over a healthy meal with friends; I simply don't need to let the food be my source of entertainment. I enjoy the food I eat, but I enjoy the rest of my life, too.

Does that mean my exact diet will also work for you? Yes, most likely. But maybe not. There's only one way to know for sure: test it out yourself. You can emulate my diet for 10 days and see how it makes you feel, see what aspects work for you. Or try any one aspect for 10 days: go without meat or bread or processed foods, add green drink or fresh juice or daily exercise, and notice the changes. I'm certain you can do anything for 10 days. See how those changes make you feel, adjust accordingly.

Improving one's health is the foundation of living a meaningful life. Without your health, nothing else matters. Truth be told, I don't care what you eat or how you exercise; I'm not looking to convert anyone to my way of eating. I don't care if you're a vegetarian or a vegan or a primal-paleo-whatever. None of these labels apply to my own dietary lifestyle, and arguing the particulars is silly anyway. What I do care about is how you feel. I want you to feel great so you can better enjoy your life and contribute beyond yourself.

Oh, and never getting sick sure is a nice bonus.

18 Minute Minimalist Exercises

True Story: I Used to be Horribly Out of Shape

A couple years ago, I couldn't do a single push-up. And I certainly couldn't do a pull-up. Hell, I didn't exercise at all. Or, when I did exercise, it was sporadic; it never lasted more than a few days before I gave up. Sound familiar?

Even after losing seventy pounds—which was due mostly to diet—I was in terrible shape. At age twenty-eight, I was doughy and flabby and weak.

But not anymore. At age thirty, I'm in the best shape of my life. That's a weird thing to say, I know—but it's the truth. I'm in good shape because I've found ways to enjoy exercising; I've found ways to make exercise a daily reward instead of a dreaded, tedious task.

Three Reasons Exercise Is Enjoyable Now

I do only exercises I enjoy. I don't enjoy running, so I don't do it. I attempted it for six months and discovered it wasn't for me. If you see me running, call the police, because someone is chasing me. Instead, I find other ways to do cardio: I walk; I get on the elliptical machine at the gym; I do bodyweight exercises that incorporate cardio.

Exercise relieves stress. Although I enjoy exercising most in the mornings, I love hitting the gym (or the park) in the evenings if I feel tense or stressed. Exercising at the end of a long, stressful day also gives me time in solitude to reflect on what's important.

Variety keeps exercise fresh. When I first started exercising, I used to hit the gym three times a week, which was certainly better than not exercising at all. Then, as I got more serious, I started going to the gym daily. This routine became horrifically time consuming, and doing the same thing over and over eventually caused me to plateau. These days I mix it up: I walk every day, and I still hit the gym occasionally, but the thing that has made the biggest, most noticeable difference has been the variety of my daily eighteen-minute bodyweight exercises.

My 18-Minute Exercises

I know, eighteen minutes sounds like an arbitrary number—that's because it is. When I started these (mostly) bodyweight exercises, I didn't have a specific window of time in mind. But I timed myself for a week and discovered that almost every time I hit the park for my exercises, I was worn out within eighteen minutes. Thus, these are my eighteen-minute exercises.

I usually alternate between the following exercises. You can of course pepper in your own favorite exercises. And, yes, these exercises are suitable for men *and* women.

Push-ups. Like I said, two years ago I couldn't do a single push-up. Eventually, I could do one (after doing modified pushups for a while). After a while, I could do ten and then twenty. Now I can do a hundred or so. I tend to do three to five sets, resulting in about 200–400 push-ups within my eighteen minutes.

Pull-ups. Two years ago I thought I'd never be able to do a pull-up. Eventually, I learned how to do one. Soon I could do two pull-ups and then four. I can do roughly 30 in a row now. I complete three to four sets, resulting in about a hundred pull-ups within my eighteen minutes. I use monkey bars at the park. You can use a pull-up bar at home. My friend Leo Babauta uses tree branches. I used to hate pull-ups, but now it's my favorite exercise.

Squats. I just started doing bodyweight squats, and I've already noticed a huge difference. I'm doing only three or four sets of 20 right now, but I'll continue to work my way up; I'll continue to grow.

Shoulder presses. I use two thirty-pound dumbbells for shoulder presses. You can use smaller or larger weights, or any random object with a little weight (e.g., a large bag of rice, a couple gallons of water, etc.). I tend to do three or four sets, resulting in about 50 shoulder presses.

I don't have a specific routine or plan, I simply take a thirty-second break between sets, bouncing from one exercise to the next. After 18 minutes, I'm spent. And I feel great afterwards. I get that incredible, tired feeling you get after a great workout. What used to be tedious is now exhilarating.

You can work your way up, even if you can't do a single pull-up or push-up. Everyone has eighteen minutes a day to focus on his or her health, right?

PART THREE

GOALS

What Is My Outcome?

It is not ambition that sets a man apart; it is the distance he is prepared to go.

I've accomplished a lot in my 31 years on this earth, not because I've had the most ambitious ambitions in the world, and certainly not because I'm smarter or more skilled or better acclimated than the next guy, but because I'm willing to keep going, to keep taking action, to keep moving forward when many other men would give up, give in, or give out. When I'm tired and uninspired, that's when I know I have to shake the dust, right myself, and advance.

This type of laudable work ethic doesn't come naturally, though. It didn't for me, at least. Rather, it's a formula—what Anthony Robbins might refer to as the Ultimate Success Formula—and it works 100% of the time it's applied.

These days I avoid goals in favor of directions, but that doesn't mean I don't have a recipe for moving forward. The way I see it, you must be willing to ask yourself four questions if you want to accomplish anything. If you do this enough, as I have, it becomes habitual and you begin to do it with everything—literally *everything*—from conversations with co-workers to massive long-term goals.

1. What is my outcome?

This should be an obvious first question in any endeavor. So obvious, in fact, that we often forget to ask it; we skip ahead to questions #3 and #4, and we wonder why we're spinning our wheels.

Another way to ask this question is to ask yourself *What do I want to happen?* Do I want to lose weight? Do I want to stop fighting with my significant other? Do I want to make a billion dollars? Before you can move forward, you have to have a vision of what you want. Without a vision, people perish.

2. Why do I want this outcome?

This is the most important question of the four. So important, in fact, that you won't find satisfaction unless you can adequately answer this question with a high level of detail. Another way to ask this question is to ask yourself *What is the purpose of my outcome?* This question is the *why* behind the *what*—the purpose behind the outcome.

Your purpose gives you the leverage you need to keep going, especially when you reach a roadblock. Without this leverage, it's easy to get excited about a new idea but quickly fall flat on your face because you no longer know why you wanted your outcome in the first place (i.e., you'll lose interest). You might have that initial ambition, but you must also find enough leverage to take you the distance.

You see, sometimes we *want* a specific outcome, not knowing *why* we desire that outcome. Perhaps you want to make a billion dollars. OK fine, but why do you want to make a billion dollars? "So I can feel secure," you might say.

OK, but can't you feel secure without earning a billion dollars? Of course you can. So your real outcome in this case isn't to earn a bunch of money; your outcome is to feel secure. There's nothing wrong with earning money, but you needn't rake in an exorbitant, arbitrary sum to make you feel secure.

To put it simply, you have to be willing to change your outcome so that you have a good enough reason to see it through.

3. What actions must I take?

Once you know your outcome and why you want your outcome, you must take action. At first, it is important to take massive action, giving you the initial momentum you need to move forward. Then you must be willing to take ongoing, consistent actions until you reach your desired outcome. There's no avoiding this step; we all must take action.

Another way to ask this question is to ask yourself *What is my strategy?* And remember, *strategy* is just a fancy way to say *recipe*. Once you have a recipe, you will be able to use it time and time again to get the same result.

4. Is this working?

Alright, now you know *what* you want, *why* you want it, and you have a *strategy* to get there. Great! You're ahead of 90% of the population. But this final question is crucial.

If you take massive action and are fortunate enough to achieve your outcome right away, then the answer is simple: *Yes, my strategy is working.* But if you're not reaching your desired outcome, then you must be willing to *change your strategy*. As long as you have a strong enough purpose, you'll be willing to change your approach until you get your desired outcome, even if it means testing a thousand different routes before you reach your destination. If you're not getting what you want, change is a must. After all, doing the same thing repeatedly and expecting a different result is the definition of insanity.

When I was a kid, my mother used to say, *If at first you don't succeed, try, try again.* Unfortunately, as adults, we tend to do the opposite. We get discouraged or embarrassed or ashamed when our recipe doesn't work, and although we make it 90% of the way to our outcome, we give up. We quit. We fall short of the finish line. What's strange is that these feelings of discouragement and embarrassment are completely mental. If we fail, we look around and hope no one noticed, and we vow to never do it again. Big mistake.

We must fail. We must figure out what doesn't work so we can figure out what does. Children already know this part of the formula. Every child fails hundreds of times before she is able to walk. But what does the child do? Does she try a handful of times and then cower in embarrassment after failing? No, she continually changes her strategy, she keeps trying until she gets it right. That's what all kids do. And now nearly every person in the world can walk.

When We Need This Formula

You don't need goals to live a compelling, meaningful, purpose-driven life. And you certainly don't need goals to make you happy. But if you're not getting what you want, it's a good idea to ask yourself these four questions. They might help you clear the clutter that is obstructing your path. And you know how I feel about clutter.

Thankfully, this formula doesn't work only for large goals; it works for any situation in your life. For example, if you get into an argument with a loved one, ask yourself these same four questions. You'll quickly discover that your desired outcome isn't to *argue*; the outcome you want is something else. And once you uncover your true outcome and its purpose, you'll be able to develop a strategy to get what you want, re-evaluating your actions until you reach your outcome.

The same goes for every aspect of life: health, relationships, passion, growth, contribution. If you ask these four questions constantly, you'll uncover myriad revelations about yourself, and you'll accomplish more than you ever thought possible.

When Goals Are Important & When They Aren't

A good traveler has no fixed plans
and is not intent on arriving.

—Lao Tzu

People have all sorts of clever words to describe what they want to do: Objective. Target. Plan. Endgame. Outcome. Goal.

If you know me, then you know I used to be The Goal Guy when I was in the corporate world. I had financial goals, health goals, sales goals, vacation goals, even consumer-purchase goals (I shit you not). I had spreadsheets of goals, precisely tracking and measuring and readjusting my plans accordingly.

These days, life is different, and I no longer have goals. Instead of an arbitrary target, I prefer to have a direction in which I travel. If you're searching for a sunrise, it's important to be headed east; for a sunset, west.

I do, however, believe there was a time in my life when goals were direly important: when I was in a hole and needed to get out. Truth be told, most of my goals were ridiculously irrelevant (e.g., purchasing and accumulation goals), but a few of my goals helped immensely (e.g., getting out of debt and losing 70–80 pounds).

I liken these latter goals to escaping a crater in the middle of the desert. When I was fat and up to my eyeballs in debt, lingering in that bowl-shaped cavity beneath the ground, my goal was to break free from the sun-scorched basin and find the earth's surface.

You see, I couldn't even fathom a direction from down there; I simply needed to get out of the hole. And my goals helped me do that. (N.B. I don't want to give too much credit to the goals, as it was actually my consistent actions over time that got me out of those fat/debt craters, not the goals themselves.)

Once I found the surface, though, I no longer needed goals. I simply needed to look around and pick a direction in which to travel. There were mountains to the west, flat planes to the east, sand dunes to the south, and whispering-pine forests to the north, all blanketed by the complete sum of endless blue heavens above. If I wanted to be on the mountain, I'd need to travel west. If I wanted to get lost in the forest, I'd head north. And so on.

The nice thing about choosing a direction is that you never know what you're going to get. You might head west in search of the mountains on the horizon, but along the way find a beautiful river instead. Or you might traverse the sand dunes only to find a village a few miles from the crater behind you. Suffice it to say, you never know what's around the bend.

Once I got out of my craters, I didn't need goals to enjoy my life. My daily habits help me do that.

I discovered that sometimes it's OK to wander in the direction of your choice. And if you get lost, so what. I mean, really, would that be so bad? Once you're out of the crater, you simply need to stay out of other craters. You can always change your direction if you're unhappy.

Moving Beyond Goals

You can't manage what you don't measure. This was the corporate mantra by which I lived for a long time. And it's total bullshit.

We used to measure everything at my old job. There were 29 metrics for which we were responsible every single day (even on weekends). There was morning reporting, 3 p.m. updates, 6 p.m. updates, and end-of-day reporting.

Suffice it to say, I was consumed by numbers. I even started thinking (and *dreaming!*) in Microsoft Excel spreadsheet terms. I was acutely aware of our stats—so much so that by the fifteenth of the month I could've told you where we were going to finish the month without even glancing at a spreadsheet.

But then I realized something: It didn't really matter. The goals were never as powerful as someone's internal motivations.

You see, people work hard for two reasons: they are externally inspired to do so, or they are internally motivated to do so. Sometimes it's a combination of both.

Sure, some people can be momentarily inspired by goal attainment, but that kind of inspiration is ephemeral, that kind of inspiration doesn't last beyond the goal itself.

Conversely, intrinsic motivation—such as the desire to grow or contribute—carries on long after the goal is met. It carries on in perpetuity. External inspiration can be the trigger, but internal motivation is what fuels someone's desire. Thus, when you discover your true motivation, you don't need an arbitrary goal.

Goals are for the unmotivated. This is one of the reasons I got rid of mine—so I could focus on what's important, so I could focus on living a meaningful life, a life centered around health, relationships, passion, growth, and contribution. I don't need goals to focus on these important aspects of my life, because I'm already motivated by these values. Arbitrary goals for these areas would be irrelevant; I simply need to live my life in accordance with these values.

100 Days with No Goals

I have lived the last 100 days with no goals. And I've never been happier or felt more alive.

When I met my friend Leo Babauta—two-thousand miles from my home in Dayton, Ohio—he said there were three things that significantly changed his life: establishing habits he enjoyed, simplifying his life, and living with no goals.

I was already living the first two: I had established my pleasurable habits, I had simplified my life. But it was difficult for me to grasp the whole "no goals" thing. The thought of living a life with no goals sounded insane to me; it was counterintuitive, it was scary, it went against almost everything I had ever learned about productivity.

In my corporate life of yesteryear, I managed hundreds of people for a large corporation, an organization in which I was often considered *the* productivity guy, *the* goal guy: I met deadlines, overproduced, exceeded expectations, got results. That's why they paid me the big bucks.

I regularly had umpteen goals in various stages of completion: short-term goals, long-term goals, personal goals, business goals, health goals, financial goals, vacation goals, consumer-purchasing goals, you name it. I thought if

I crossed enough goals off my to-do list, I'd eventually be content. So I worked harder and harder, focusing on every new goal with lapidary precision.

But I was stressed out of my mind with all those goals. My hauntingly perpetual to-do list was just that—perpetual, never-ending. And it was ever-growing. Plus, I was continuously disappointed when I didn't achieve a goal, or when I missed a deadline. Hell, I was even disappointed when I attained a goal but didn't overachieve. It was a self-consuming cocaine high—it was never enough.

I needed a way to quit my goals cold turkey, so I did two things after speaking with Leo...

First, I asked myself, "why do I have these goals?" I had goals so I could tell if I was "accomplishing" what I was "supposed" to accomplish. If I met a goal, I was allowed to be happy—right? Then I thought: Wait a minute, why must I achieve a specific result towards an arbitrary goal to be happy? Why don't I just allow myself to be happy now?

Second, I decided to live with no goals for a while. I didn't know how long, because I didn't make it a goal. I figured I'd give it a shot for a month or so, maybe longer, to see what happened. If it affected me negatively, I could return to my rigid life of "achieving" and "producing results" with my color-coded spreadsheets containing scads of goals.

What happened? Breaking free from goals changed my entire outlook on life.

Three Ways Living with No Goals Changed My Life

1. I am less stressed. I have virtually no stress now. Sure, there are brief moments in which I feel vexed or bothered—but I feel so much less stress these days. People I've known for years comment on how calm I am. With no goals, they say I'm a different person—a better person.

2. I am more productive. I didn't anticipate this one. I thought getting rid of goals meant I was going to sacrifice results and productivity. But the opposite has been true. I tossed productivity and became more productive. I've written the best literary fiction of my life, I've watched our website's readership increase significantly, I've met remarkable new people, and I've been able to contribute to other people like never before. The last 100 days have been the most productive days of my life.

3. I am happier and more content. During my 30 years on this earth, I've never been this consistently happy or content. It is an incredible feeling, even surreal at times. With the decreased stress and increased productivity resulting from no goals, I am able to enjoy my life, I am able to live in the moment. And thus I am appreciably happier and more content.

Three Misconceptions About No Goals

Three arguments against the no-goal lifestyle presented themselves to me in the last 100 days, all three of which I'd like to address.

1. Complacency: Doesn't a life with no goals make you complacent? Well, if by "complacent" you mean "content," then yes. But, otherwise, no it didn't make me complacent. In fact, the opposite was true: after removing the stress from my life, I partook in new, exciting endeavors, while living a passionate, meaningful life.

2. Growth: Doesn't a life with no goals prevent you from growing? No. I've grown considerably in the last 100 days. I've gotten into the best shape of my life, strengthened my personal relationships, established new relationships, and written more than ever before. I've grown more in the last 100 days than any other 100-day period in my life.

3. You still have goals: You say you have no goals, but don't you still have some goals, like finishing your new novel or "being happy" or "living in the moment"? It's important to make a distinction here: yes, I want to "be happy" and "live in the moment" and "live a healthy life," but these are choices, not goals. I choose to be happy. I choose to live in the moment. I choose to live a healthy life. I don't need to measure these events, I simply live this way. As for my new novel, I intend to finish writing it—I've never worked harder on anything in my life—but I'm enjoying the process of writing it, and if I never finish, that's okay too. I'm not stressed about it anymore.

Living with no goals has changed me for the better. It has added layers of happiness and contentment I didn't realize were possible. It has allowed me to contribute to other people in meaningful ways. I'm not going back to a goal-oriented life. No goals. None at all. Life is outstanding without them.

PART FOUR

EXPERIMENTS

Resolving to Learn from Failure

I failed last year. A lot. I failed more times than I can count. No matter how often I fail, the fear of failure is always sharp and cutting and it never feels good.

At the beginning of 2011 I made my first ever New Year's Resolution, in which I resolved to not purchase anything for a year. It was a lofty resolution, I know. It sounded easy at the time.

Two months after making my resolution, my thought process around buying stuff had radically changed. At first, when I wanted to purchase an item I would think, *Hey, look, that thing looks cool; I think I'll buy it.*

But eventually, I was forced to face the fact that I couldn't buy those things. And by the end of the fourth month, something beautiful had happened: I no longer wanted to buy new things. My entire thought process around impulse consumption had changed.

In other words, I had accidentally reprogrammed myself.

The point of my resolution was to prove I didn't need to buy material possessions for a year. But I learned I could actually change *myself* in the process. After four months, I no longer wanted to buy stuff on impulse. The endless desire to consume was gone. It was—and still is—a phenomenal feeling.

And then, six months into the experiment, something unfortunate happened: I spilled tea all over my computer. It wouldn't power on. It was ruined. Thankfully, my first thought was not, *I guess I'll go buy another computer.* Instead, my first thought was, *How can I live without this item?*

I went the next several weeks without a computer. I wrote essays longhand on yellow legal pads. I wrote fiction by hand and it looked like the musings of a madman. I accessed the Internet at libraries, at friends houses, anywhere except my tea-soaked MacBook.

After a few weeks, Ryan offered to give me a new laptop for my thirtieth birthday, an offer I turned down because I felt like it was cheating. So I soldiered on, computerless for several more weeks.

Eventually I realized I was less productive without my computer. I was writing less, I wasn't enjoying writing as much, and I didn't feel as good about what I was writing. I realized that I was depriving myself of an essential tool. For me, minimalism has never been about deprivation. Rather, minimalism is about getting rid of life's excess in favor of the essential. For me, a computer was essential, so I bought a new one.

And throughout the rest of the year, I bought a few other tools I needed as well. But I never went back to the impulse-driven consumption of yesteryear. I was reprogrammed. And I will be forever changed by the experience of not buying stuff this year. I strongly recommend not buying anything for the next four months. Give it a shot. See what it does to your impulses.

At the end of the day, my experiment was a failure. But it was a beautiful failure that I'm incredibly thankful for.

This year's resolution? Well, I don't have any goals, but I plan to continue to learn from my failures.

How about you?

Pushing Through Frustration: Going Phoneless

Whenever I make a big change in my life, I tend to get frustrated.

When I got rid of television, the first few weeks were frustrating. When I killed the Internet at home, the first month was frustrating. When I stopped buying material possessions for a year, the first four months were frustrating. When I changed my diet and started exercising daily, the first six months were frustrating.

Eventually the frustration turns into reward; the pain becomes pleasure. This process is gradual, but it happens. The key for me has been finding ways to push through the initial frustration—pushing through the pain, knowing pleasure is just around the bend.

In the end, tomorrow's pleasure drastically outweighs the ephemeral pain of today.

And now, for my next magic trick, I'm getting rid of my smartphone for a couple months while I focus on rewriting my novel. In fact, I'll have no phone at all. No landline, no Skype, no cheap cellphone.

I'm not a Luddite. I don't think there's anything

inherently wrong with TV, Internet at home, cellphones, or technology in general (all these things can be wonderful tools in our lives). Rather, I want to get rid of unnecessary distractions so I can be more productive, focus on what's most important, and better enjoy my life. More important, I want to see what effect this change will have on my psyche. Every drastic change I've made, good or bad, has had a profound effect on the way I see my life—my perspective today is radically different than yesterday's perspective.

My lack of a telephone also means my face-to-face interactions with my friends will become more meaningful. Dinner or coffee or a walk through Dayton will mean so much more because we won't have the luxury of updating each other with every banal detail of our lives via text message or a five-minute phone call. Every interaction will be an opportunity for us to live in the moment, to be on the mountain.

But what about emergencies? Truth be told, I can't possibly plan for every emergency. It's fear that makes us try to plan for every potential pothole. My neighbors have a phone if I really need one. My local coffee shop has Internet when I need to get online. My friends will still be able to contact me via email. I'll still be able to update social media when I'm on the Internet.

So many people have told me, *I could never give up my cellphone*. I used to say the same thing. The truth is, *yes they could*, but they choose to not live without. There's nothing wrong with that choice, but realize you can do anything you want to do. Sometimes you just need to make the change and push through the initial frustration.

Reprogramming the Twitch

Must one unplug from reality to properly observe reality?

Going without a phone for any extended period of time seems to be the modern day equivalent of a vow of silence. Two months ago I decided to 86 my phone for sixty days as an experiment, just to see what would happen, just to see if my world would keep spinning. People were shocked. Some were appalled. Some people were worried about me.

I'll skip the overused Matrix references about unplugging from the grid and simply say that I learned more about myself than I intended to. I couldn't've done so without disconnecting for a while, without stepping back and actually thinking about my life in a deliberate, uninterrupted way.

This is what I learned during my two months of quiet time.

We have weird expectations. I realized I needed to get rid of my cellphone for a while when I felt pressure to respond to text messages, email, and social media throughout the day. We all have different expectations. You might expect someone to respond to a text message in an hour, someone else might expect a response in ten minutes, another person might expect a response the same day. These expectations are arbitrary. When I eliminated my ability to immediately respond, I was able to toss everyone's expectations into the ocean.

Meaningful conversations. Without the banality of ephemeral text conversations, my real face-to-face conversations have become more meaningful. While I'm with my close friends now, I have more to talk about. Ergo, we enjoy our conversations more.

People are supportive and understanding. When we make changes in our lives, we're often afraid of what people will think of us. *Will they think I'm crazy or stupid or out of touch?* The truth is, people are more supportive and understanding than we think. Particularly the people who are closest to us. Especially when we discuss our changes with them and let them know we're making those changes so we can live happier lives.

We program ourselves. Without knowing it, our daily activities have a profound impact on our future selves. I used to reach for my BlackBerry every few minutes no matter where I was—even at the urinal. Even when the phone wasn't with me I would reach for it. I was programmed to do so. I call this the Twitch.

We can reprogram ourselves. Similarly, we can change these patterns. When we remove a habit from our lives, we become acutely aware of how that habit affected us. This is true for any habit: smoking, over-eating, etc. It took 22 days for me to reprogram the Twitch, 22 days of pausing and noticing why I was Twitching. After those 22 days I no longer felt the urge to immediately react; I no longer felt the need to pacify myself with transitory activities like texting or responding to emails during every moment of "downtime."

Downtime is a misnomer. We used to have precious interstitial zones in which we could find momentary solace: airports, checkout lines, waiting rooms, and other places were transient sanctuaries in which we could bask in reverie. This is no longer the case. I now notice everyone on their phones during these precious moments. They are attempting to be more productive or interactive, but I've discovered that stopping and thinking during these moments is far more productive than fiddling with my phone.

The world goes on. Without a cellphone, without the Internet, without a TV, the world keeps turning. You can test anything for a short period of time to see if it's right for you. It's not that hard to give up anything when you live in the real world. In all honesty, there wasn't a single time when I actually *needed* my phone in the last two months. Sure, there were times when it was inconvenient, times when I had to fight through the frustration, but that was a small price to pay to reprogram the Twitch.

Yes, I'll go back to using a cellphone for practical purposes—GPS, necessary phone calls, the Dictionary app I missed dearly, a memo pad, and a few other useful apps—but I'll use it utterly differently going forward. I'm not going to use it to check email anymore, I'm not going to use it to send text messages while standing at a urinal, and I'm not going to rely on it as my primary means of interacting with the world around me. My cellphone usage will be more intentional than it was before. My phone will be a tool, not an appendage.

Photoless Vacations

I'm living inside the moment,
not taking pictures to save it
—Drake, "The Resistance"

Imagine yourself reaching for your camera-phone as the sun sets beneath billowing clouds, a smear of pale pink on the horizon. You take a picture. And then another. And then another.

We all want to capture the moment. We desire to preserve it forever, salvaging the beauty of everything we see. So we grab our cellphones, our iPads, our digital cameras, and *SNAP!* we take a few photos to safeguard our memories.

Sounds harmless, right? I mean, look around, everyone's doing it. You can't go to a monument or a concert or even a sunset without scads of pedestrians fiddling with their electronics, trying to save and share the experience.

There seems to be two problems with this incessant picture-taking behavior, and I myself have been an accomplice to said problem for way too long.

First, by fumbling around with my device, looking for

the best angle and filter, snapping the picture, viewing the picture, and then often retaking the shot in an effort to get the "right" photo, I'm missing the actual moment. My desire to capture the moment actually *ruins* the moment. It makes it less beautiful, less real, and in many ways less photo-worthy.

Second, the "result" is artificial. Time doesn't happen in this kind of take-and-retake way. We don't get to re-do the experiences of our lives. And yet we take our pictures as if we can "get it just right." It gives us a false sense of security, a sense that we can not only change the moment, but somehow save only its best parts. The fact of the matter is that the best parts exist because of the worst parts, not despite them. We cannot enjoy life's mountains without its valleys.

> *Didn't have a camera by my side this time*
> *Hoping I would see the world through both my eyes*
> *Today I finally overcame,*
> *trying to fit the world inside a picture frame*
> *You should have seen that sunrise with your own eyes*
> *It brought me back to life*
> —John Mayer, "3×5"

Thus, during the last leg of our meetup tour, I avoided reaching for my phone to take pictures. And even though I was conscious about this choice, I slipped up a few times. Every beautiful sunset, every Wyoming sky, every rushing

Montana river, brought with it The Twitch, an urge to reach for my camera-phone and seize the picturesque setting. But I resisted, and after an instant of hesitation, I was able to enjoy each event for all its worth, not attempting to put a piece of it in my pocket to save for later. I took it all in, right then, right there, enjoying the experience for what it was: a perfect moment.

Don't get me wrong; I think photography is a beautiful art form. And when they're done well, photos are breathtaking. Furthermore, we're a visual culture, and so pictures play a large role in the way we communicate. I'm not going to stop taking photos altogether, but I am going to remain more cognizant of my surroundings. I'm going to enjoy the experience first and embrace the impermanence of the moment. And if an unobtrusive opportunity arises to snap a single photo, then I will. Maybe. Or maybe not. It's okay to be on the mountain—to be meditative—without proving to everyone else you were there to see it.

What If You Accidentally Spilled Bleach on Half Your Wardrobe?

What if you spilled bleach on half your wardrobe? What would you do?

Some hypothetical questions are so ridiculous that we often dismiss them as absurd, laughable queries. Sadly, though, the above question is *not* purely hypothetical.

Last week, after returning from our book tour, fatigued and murky-headed from cross-country traversing, I separated my dirty laundry into ordinal piles, prepping each color-coded assemblage for its usual rinse and spin cycles. Then, unknowingly and stupidly, I spilled a bottle of liquid bleach on literally half the clothes, staining the floor-strewn heaps, instantly ruining the majority of my wardrobe.

I was shocked by two things.

First, I was shocked by my own brainlessness. How could I make such a ridiculous mistake? Truth be told, I simply wasn't paying attention. There's no other explanation. If there's a lesson to be learned here, it's that *attention must be paid*, even during the most mundane tasks.

Second, I was shocked that I wasn't more horrified by my own idiotic mistake. I mean, I should be outraged, right?

Hell, two years ago I would've been pissed; I would have fumed angrily and cursed the ceiling and hurled various breakable objects at one or more of my apartment walls. But last week, as sodium hypochlorite soaked through my threads, I didn't react obnoxiously. Instead, I realized that I couldn't control everything. I took a few deep breaths, snatched a mop from my closet, and started cleaning up the mess I'd made, recognizing that the sooner we clean up our own mess, the sooner we can move on with life.

Sure, half my attire is ruined, but everything's fine. I'll replace some of the clothes if I need to, but my closet isn't upset and nor should I be. Those clothes were just clothes—replaceable things that don't have any more meaning than the meaning I give to them. There's no use in crying over spilt milk, or, in this case, spilt bleach.

Check Email Like a Minimalist

Most of us receive a multitude of emails each day. It's easy to address them one by one, filtering and sorting and replying to them as they tumble into our inboxes.

Most of the emails I receive are either positive or pointless—nice words from readers (positive) or junk mail that I do my best to filter out of my life (pointless). Thus, it's only logical to want to check my email frequently, receiving textual praise while clearing the clutter. It's a win-win, right? After all, who doesn't want constant positive feedback? And who doesn't want to *feel* productive?

This sounds ideal, except for one problem: we have real lives.

You see, living in our inboxes—something I did for a long time, especially during my 12 years in the corporate world—forces us to be on edge, always seeking the next nugget of digital applause, always anticipating the next question, the next "follow-up," the next "action item." Worse, it keeps me away from living a fulfilling life, one that doesn't revolve around the white glow of my computer screen.

The problem with email is that it's never enough. Even when we whittle our incoming messages down to zero, we're constantly waiting for the next fleeting bit of good information. I call these bits "food pellets from the universe."

Similar to a lab rat, we have trained ourselves to click that "get mail" button to receive these food pellets. Hit the lever, get the food. Hit the lever, get the food. Hit the lever, get the food. Sometimes the food is tasty—a kind message from a friend, a thoughtful question, a hilarious link from Nicodemus. But most of the time these food pellets are filled with empty calories and they taste like cardboard.

So instead of checking my email throughout each day, I check it once a day at most, and some days I don't check it at all. A handful of changes in my life have made this shift possible—and far less stressful than you might think...

Home. I don't have Internet at home. This one change, albeit utterly frustrating at first, is likely the most productive thing I've ever done. Because I don't have Internet at home, it is impossible for emails to penetrate the walls of my abode.

Phone. I don't get emails on my phone. Once I brought my BlackBerry back into my life—after going two months without it—I discovered that it was better and far less stressful to remove email from my phone altogether. Now I use my phone to text, tweet, and (ahem) talk.

Planning. When I check my email, I do so deliberately. I set aside a block of time, clear my plate, and embrace the messages on my schedule, on my terms, when it's convenient for me. If I do it right, it's possible to live in the moment, even when I'm checking my email.

Inbox Minimalism. I've applied many of my friend Ethan's inbox minimalism principles to my email account, drastically cutting down the superfluous stuff staggering into my inbox (more info available at themins.com/inbox).

Expectations. It's important to set the proper expectations with people. Let people know how you feel about email (they likely feel the same way). Ask them to respect your time and attention. My friends know that I don't like receiving superfluous emails, and if they must send me an email, then I likely won't respond right away. My students know that I don't respond the same day either—though I commit to responding to them within 72 hours. When I do respond, it's thoughtful, succinct, and, above all, value-adding. The best question to ask yourself before clicking the send button is, *Does this email add value?*

PART FIVE

CLUTTER

The Short Guide to Getting Rid of Your Crap

Yay, it's Friday! Time to head home and relax after a week of hard work.

1. Enter the front door of your home. Toss off your shoes. Notice, lying beneath, a pair of boots you have worn only once. Shrug.

2. Turn on the television and sit on your IKEA couch. Attempt to relax. Awaken 20 minutes later, realizing that you've been passively flipping through channels. Turn off the TV, remove the batteries from your remote. Toss them in your Blendtec blender. Stop yourself moments away from doing something drastic.

3. Briefly fondle the iPhone in your pocket. Stop yourself, realizing you were about to do the exact same thing with Reddit as you just did with TV. Call and cancel your data plan in the nick of time.

4. Begin to wonder what people did before television and

Internet access. Observe the room around you, looking over the unread books and unwatched DVDs lining your dusty shelves. Consider shopping, then picture the unworn clothes occupying your cavernous walk-in closet.

5. Realize your imagination has turned all black and grey.

6. Suddenly recognize that you haven't used your "spare" room…ever. Shit! Do the math and realize said room is costing you five or six hours of work per month. Take out a piece of paper and compare it to that trip to Japan you've been meaning to take. Stare at the math in disbelief. Stuff the paper in your mouth and begin to chew.

7. Realize that the brief emotional rush that accompanied the purchase of each item in your home is now gone, leaving only the object itself in its most basic, uninteresting form. The gorgeous, pastel designer couch has become simply a chair. A beautiful glass buffet is transformed into a mere table. A set of immaculate handmade dishes has aged into nothing but a bunch of plates. Your goose down duvet is actually just a blanket. Wince.

8. Glance down at your groceries and realize that the Doritos, Lay's, and Ruffles you purchased are all just colored corn and potatoes.

9. Open your credit card bill. Wide-eyed, discover how often you've confused shopping with actual extra-curricular activities. Consider joining a monastery.

10. Remember that time you went over to a party in a friend's pseudo-abandoned loft. Recall the roommates, the self-made art and photos on the walls, the obscenely cheap rent, and the embraced simplicity.

11. Begin to make a quick list of the top 10 things you own in terms of how much they cost. With horror, make a second list of the top 10 things that make you happy. Sense the creeping dread as you realize there is no overlap between the two at all. Shudder in terror.

12. Decide to have a packing party like your friend suggested one time. Take the old sheets you never used from Crate & Barrel. Cover all your stuff with them. Endeavor not to uncover it unless you decide you need to use it. Realize suddenly that you would never use anything at all because you are never actually home.

13. Remember a time in childhood when you were more excited by ideas, love, travel, and people than by anything else. Realize that you have, somehow, bought into a new religion, and that malls, from the inside, look exactly like cathedrals.

14. Consider starting a fire.

15. Consider that, perhaps, you are more than just your stuff. Begin to take a long walk. Breathe.

16. Begin to relax. Give yourself the freedom to begin to dream again.

Essay written in collaboration with my friend, New York Times *bestselling author Julien Smith of InOverYourHead.net.*

Learning to Let Go

"Everything I've ever let go of has claw marks on it."
—David Foster Wallace

A sunset is beautiful, but it lasts only so long. Once it's over, it's over.

In time, perfection is tainted by life's beautiful blemishes, and every perfectionist dies a thousand deaths. We often look at the things we enjoy—the relationships, the experiences, the possessions—and we want to hold on to them forever. We expect that these things will continue to add the same value to our lives, day in and day out.

But life does not work this way. Not everything that adds value today will add value tomorrow.

This is particularly evident within our material possessions. Each time we purchase a sparkling new thingamabob, we bask in the light of its potential, excited by the initial value the new object brings to our lives. Over time, though, the value wanes, the glossy newness wears off, and our excitement abruptly dissipates.

When that possession stops adding value, however, what do we do? Do we ask ourselves why? Do we donate it or sell it or question why we purchased it in the first place? Not usually.

Often, once the dullness sets in, we let our effects gather dust or wither away in boxes in our basements, closets, and junk drawers. Out of sight, out of mind.

And but then the only way to reclaim the missing value is to find another thingamajig that is shiny and exciting and new. This cycle is a dangerous downward spiral, a vortex of consumption in which we're constantly looking for that next nugget of excitement, that next burst of euphoria, that cocaine high that doesn't last but a few feet past the cash register.

Thankfully, there are at least two ways to break this vicious cycle.

First, we must question our new purchases. Of course there's nothing inherently wrong with material possessions. What's wrong is the idea that material possessions will bring lasting joy and contentment. They won't. Instead, we must ask, Will this thing add value to my life? and Is this thing still adding value to my life? This kind of intentional living, when done consistently, will form lasting, empowering habits.

Second, we must be willing to let go. We should let go of superfluous things in our lives, starting with the dusty belongings inhabiting every nook and cranny and dark corner of our homes, eventually moving on to the more difficult things no longer adding value to our lives: sentimental items, unnecessarily large homes, the American Dream, extra cars, shitty relationships.

Ultimately, we must learn to let go. To do so, acceptance

is the key. We needn't settle, but we all have a reality we must accept. As much as we might want to, we'll never be able to hold on to a sunset. Likewise, we can't retain every thing and still lead meaningful lives. Life is fulfilling only when we allow ourselves to let go, when we allow ourselves to be in the moment, when we allow ourselves to feel the moment. After all, this moment is life's only true reality.

How I Got Rid of 2,000 Books and Started Reading More

I used to own 2,000 books. Slightly more than that, actually. I had all kinds of books: hard covers, paperbacks, trade paperbacks, literary fiction, writing and grammar books, books of photography, self-help books, my dead father's collection of old medical journals, genre fiction, those cute little pop-up books, you name it.

I had shelves and shelves and more shelves of books, some of which I'd actually read, and many of which I'd read *someday*; you know, whenever I got around to it. Who was I kidding?

I thought my overflowing shelves of books made me look important and intelligent and cool. *Look at me, I know how to read—a lot!*

What's worse, I thought these books made me somebody. They were a part of my identity. Thus, those books were a part of me. And once something's a part of your identity—once it becomes a part of *you*—it's incredibly hard to shed.

This is true for anything we incorporate into our identities—our careers, our cars, our homes, our possessions, our sentimental items, our silly DVD collections. These things become part of us, and they become incredibly pernicious anchors in our lives, anchors that keep us at bay, away from the freedom of the open seas.

Ironically, three quotes from a particular book I owned —Chuck Palahniuk's *Fight Club*—are what inspired me to get rid of the vast majority of my books a little over a year ago:

"Reject the basic assumptions of civilization, especially the importance of material possessions."

"The things you own end up owning you."

"It's only after we've lost everything that we're free to do anything."

These words resonated with me deeply. I could feel on my nerve-endings what Palahniuk was saying. I read those quotes several times and within a week sold or donated 98% of my books. I purchased a Kindle and kept one shelf of my favorite physical books.

Then, last month I got rid of those books too. I kept the four grammar books I'm using to teach my online writing class, all four of which I reference regularly, but that's it.

Some older books aren't yet on Kindle, which is a shame. In those rare cases, I'll get the book elsewhere, and when I'm done reading it, I'll donate it.

Now, I no longer own piles of books, but I read more than before. I enjoy each book, taking them in slowly, absorbing the knowledge, processing the information, contemplating their lessons. But I needn't retain the physical book to get value from its words.

Think about it. How much value was I placing in those dusty 2,000 books I owned. Obviously, it was far more than their real value. The real value was in the words—in the action of reading—not in the physical books themselves.

There is no value in having a room full of books you don't need—especially when other people can get value from those books. You're so much more than your stuff. Even when you're in an empty room, the value is within you, not your things.

Digital Clutter Is Different from Physical Clutter

Digital clutter isn't nearly as problematic as physical clutter. Don't believe me? Then try to move 2,000 books to a new residence.

First, box up the physical books, taking them off their shelves one by one, labeling each box with its appropriate label (self-help, literary fiction, Cambodian interpretive dance, etc.); then carry them to your vehicle, box by box, being careful not to drop them; and then haul them to your new home, carry them inside, carefully unpack each box, and re-shelve each individual book until every last book is (sort of) back where it was before you started this whole tedious exercise.

Then, next time you move, instead of boxing up all those books, grab your Kindle with all 2,000 titles, toss it into your bag, and be on your merry little way.

It's not hard to realize which method is easier. I've done both. And I threw my back out (literally) while going through the first exercise. Shockingly, the Kindle exercise didn't have the same savage effect on my lumbar musculature.

That said, digital clutter can still be a significant problem. At *The Minimalists*, we advocate digitizing your physical items whenever you can, especially with those old CDs, DVDs, photos, and files of paperwork you hardly ever need.

Getting these items out of the way is a monumental first step. But we also recommend constantly paring down your digital "stuff" as well. It's important to keep your digital stuff —your email inbox, your files, your music, your collection of recently downloaded cute cat videos—organized to save you time.

And it's equally as important to get rid of files you no longer need. The rule of thumb I use is *the last six months*. That is, if I haven't needed something in the last six months —saved documents, old college papers, Ryan's "secret" recipe for Rice Crispy Treats—then I get rid of it. I do this twice a year; it takes me less than an hour each time I purge my files.

As with any rule, there are exceptions. For example, taxes should obviously be kept for seven years (or longer depending on where you live). But these exceptions are few and far between.

As for pictures, you needn't delete any photos: you can use them every day if you have a digital picture frame. (We show you the best way to scan all those pictures hiding in albums in your basement on our website: themins.com/day14)

You might be addressing your physical clutter, which is great. But when's the last time you purged your digital clutter?

Deleting the Music You No Longer Listen To

Are you actually going to listen to that Ricky Martin album again? Then why is it still on your iPod? Why do you keep music you haven't listened to in years? Do you keep it *just in case*?

I certainly used to.

Once upon a time, I owned more than 2,000 CDs. This is no surprise to the people who know me well. I'm an auditory learner—which is the reason why most of my writing has a run-on-ish, out-loud, tumbling-words auditory pace and cadence—and music has played a significant role in shaping my life.

Because my music was important to me—because it added immense value to my life—I transferred all my CDs (literally all 2,000 of them) one by one to my iTunes library, until my full-belly hard drive was bloated with more than 20,000 songs, from A-HA (hey, no laughing!) to ZZ Top and everything in-between.

Music is a special art form. It's different than movies or television or even books. Music is created to be consumed more than once, absorbed over time, shaping itself to your conscious after many listens. Movies and books are generally created to be consumed once (maybe twice), not repeatedly.

That's why I advocate getting rid of old movies and old books.

But today, I'd also like you to consider getting rid of some of your music.

Recently, I deleted 80% of the music in my iTunes library. How did I select what to delete? I spent a few hours shuffling through my albums, starting at the top (yes, if you're wondering, A-HA was the first to go). I deleted *everything* I hadn't listened to in the last six months. Billy Joel: gone. Guns 'N' Roses: gone. Cory Hart: mostly gone, although "Sunglasses at Night" is still there. *What?*

All that's left is the good stuff—the music I enjoy listening to. Now, my iTunes library is easier to navigate, it's clutterfree, and it's filled with music I love: The National, David Gray, Talib Kweli, et al.

How much of your music is in the way of the good stuff?

Email for Minimalists

Email of Yesteryear

I manage my email vastly differently than I used to.

When I worked in corporate America, I would get 150 to 250 emails a day. The first thing I did in the morning was reach for my BlackBerry and check my inbox. I was anchored to that BlackBerry throughout the day, checking it every five or ten minutes, always anticipating every new message. It was an unspoken corporate expectation—to be on call, always available.

And at night, before my head hit the pillow, the last thing I did—out of habit—was check my BlackBerry for new messages. Looking back on it, it seems a bit crazy now, but, at the time, that was the expectation, and thus it felt completely normal.

The truth is that less than 40 of those 150 to 250 emails actually required any kind of action. Some of them just needed to be read and filed away mentally. Others were irrelevant but still required my precious time to read and decide whether or not it was pertinent information.

To manage such a daunting load, I developed an elaborate system to organize the chaos—constantly checking my inbox, filing messages into appropriate "to do" folders, delegating tasks to various employees, and setting priorities for various actions I needed to take. It was a vicious cycle, and I was never "caught-up." I couldn't, by definition, ever be caught-up with such a barrage of perpetual incoming info. But I soldiered on—reading, filing, prioritizing, delegating, and taking action to get things done.

Email Today

The picture looks much different for me today…

Size doesn't matter. I don't subscribe to the five-sentences email philosophy prescribed by some of my friends. I like long emails if they are clever, well thought out, and add value to my life (that last part is the most important). For some emails, however, five sentences is way too long. And most emails shouldn't be sent at all. Besides, I'm perfectly capable of writing a two-page 715-word sentence that would render this rule irrelevant. So, instead of limiting myself, I think twice before I send an email. Is there a better way to communicate this info?

Use your smartphone as a tool. I still get about the same amount of emails (thanks to the success of our website), and I still have a BlackBerry. But my BlackBerry works for me, not the other way around. It is a tool I use to respond when a computer isn't nearby. If I'm writing, I leave it in the other room. If I'm on tour, I use it for short responses while I'm traveling. If I'm spending time with a friend, I leave it in my pocket or, better yet, at home or in my car.

Unsubscribe if you don't find value. My email is my central hub, it's what I use to aggregate all my incoming info (comments, communications, websites, newsletters, blogs, etc.). If something is no longer adding value to my life, I unsubscribe.

Don't respond to email every day. If you send me an email, you *will* get a response (if it warrants one), but that response is on my terms, on my timeline. No one should send an email to anyone and expect an immediate reply. Life is too precious to spend our days feeling anxious with required email responses.

Don't act on everything. Not every email requires an action. In fact, most don't. Sometimes it's OK to just hit *delete*.

Delete nearly everything. I used to archive all my messages, but now I just delete them when I'm done reading. It's incredibly freeing. *But what if you realize you need something you deleted?* Well, I save the few messages I'm certain I'll want to reference later—I save those messages in a folder and I delete everything else. I have the trash set to keep everything I delete for 30 days before the messages are gone. But, in reality, I've learned to let go. If something gets lost, it's not the end of the world. I'm more concerned about the future than the past.

How could you manage your email differently?

When Everything Is Your Favorite Thing

When you get rid of most of your stuff, your life invariably changes. Without all the things in your way, you have the opportunity to focus on the most important aspects of your life.

Once I jettisoned the superfluous stuff in my life, I was able to focus on my health, cultivate meaningful relationships, get into the best shape of my life, grow as an individual, and contribute beyond myself in myriad ways.

But there was also an unexpected benefit from my newly uncluttered life: now I truly enjoy everything I own.

Before I embraced minimalism, I had a lot of stuff: A three bedroom house teeming with stuff. A basement and a two-car garage filled with boxes overflowing with stuff. Spare bedrooms and closets and cabinets jam-packed with stuff. Every nook, every cranny—more stuff.

It was hard to keep track of it all. And, to be honest, all that stuff added very little value to my life. Often, it just made me feel anxious and overwhelmed and even depressed.

I was unhappy with the way I felt, so I started questioning everything I owned.

Today I don't own much, but the things I do own add

immense value to my life. When I got rid of my extraneous material possessions, what remained were the things I use every day.

Now nearly everything I own is my *favorite* thing. All my clothes are my favorite clothes. All my furniture is my favorite furniture. All my possessions are my favorite possessions—all of which I'm able to enjoy every day of my life.

How about you? What if you enjoyed *everything* you owned? How would it make you feel if you were surrounded by your favorite things every day?

PART SIX

RELATIONSHIPS

Letting Go of Shitty Relationships

Some relationships are incredibly pernicious. We often develop relationships out of convenience, without considering the traits necessary to build a successful bond with another person—important traits like unwavering support and shared trust and loving encouragement.

When a relationship is birthed out of convenience or proximity or chemistry alone, it is bound to fail. We need more than a person's physical presence to maintain a meaningful connection, but we routinely keep people around because … well, simply because they're already *around.*

It's easy to develop a connection with a coworker or a schoolmate or someone who's always there—even when they're not adding any real value to our lives. And it's even easier to stay in those relationships. That's because old relationships are convenient, and starting new relationships is difficult—it requires work. But so does anything worth holding on to.

We've all at some point held on to someone who didn't deserve to be there. And most of us still have someone in our lives who continually drains us: Someone who doesn't add value. Someone who isn't supportive. Someone who takes and takes and takes without giving back to the relationship. Someone who contributes very little and prevents us from growing. Someone who constantly plays the victim.

But victims become victimizers. And these people are dangerous. They keep us from feeling fulfilled. They keep us from living meaningful lives. Over time, these negative relationships become part of our identity—they define us, they become *who we are.*

Fortunately, this needn't be the case. Several actions can be taken to rid ourselves of negative relationships.

First, you can attempt to fix the relationship. This is obviously the preferable solution (albeit not always possible or worthwhile). People change over time, and so do relationships. You can change how your relationship works —be it marriage, friendship, or family—without completely ditching the relationship.

Sit down with the person who's draining the vitality from your life and explain to them what must change in order for your relationship to work. Explain that you need them to be more supportive, that you need them to participate in your growth, that they are important to you, but the relationship in its current state does not make you happy. Explain that you're not attempting to change them as a person; you simply want to change how your relationship works.

Finally, ask them what they'd like to change about the relationship. Ask them how you can add more value. Listen attentively, act accordingly.

Or, if you're unable to change the relationship, you can

end it altogether. This is incredibly difficult, but it applies to any relationship: family, friends, lovers, coworkers, acquaintances. If someone is doing nothing but draining your life, it's perfectly acceptable to tell them, "This relationship is no longer right for me, so I must end it—I must move on."

It's OK to move on. You owe it to yourself to move on. You owe it to yourself to be happy with the relationships you have. You are in control.

Moving on is sometimes the only way to develop new, empowering relationships. Starting anew, empty-handed and full-hearted, you can build fresher, stronger, more supportive relationships—important relationships that allow you to have fun and be happy and contribute beyond yourself. These are the meaningful relationships we all need.

It's also important to do your part. You too must add value to the relationship. Not by buying gifts or commoditizing your love, but by showing up every day and rigorously exhibiting how much you care, demonstrating your love through consistent actions, continually going out of your way to help the other person grow.

You see, both people must do their part to grow the relationship. Only then will both of you be satisfied with the relationship you've built.

The Commodification of Love

There's another holiday lurking somewhere around the corner. Valentine's Day. Mother's Day. Sweetest Day. Birthdays. Christmas. We've programmed ourselves to give and receive gifts on these and many other holidays to show our love for one another.

We've even been told that gift-giving is one of our "love languages." This idea is utterly ridiculous, and yet we treat it as gospel: I love you—see, here's this expensive shiny thing I bought you.

Gift-giving is not a love language any more than Pig Latin is a Romance language. Rather, gift-giving is a vapid, pernicious cultural imperative in our society, and we've bought it (literally) hook, line, and sinker. We've become consumers of love.

The grotesque idea that we can somehow commodify love is nauseating. Buying diamonds is not evidence of everlasting devotion. Commitment, trust, understanding— these are indications of devotion.

Gift-giving is by definition transactional. But love is not a transaction. Love is transcendent; it transcends language and material possessions and can be shown only by our thoughts, actions, and intentions.

Perhaps Jonathan Franzen said it best: "Love is about bottomless empathy, born out of the heart's revelation that another person is every bit as real as you are. To love a specific person, and to identify with his or her struggles and joys as if they were your own, you have to surrender some of your self."

This doesn't mean there's something necessarily wrong with buying a gift for someone, though I recommend gifting experiences over material possessions. But don't fool yourself by associating that gift with love; love doesn't work that way.

PART SEVEN

CHANGES

A Single Tweet Changed My Life

I never asked for this. I stumbled into minimalism serendipitously and haphazardly, not knowing what I was looking for. It was utterly unintentional at first.

The year was 2009, early autumn. As the leaves resisted their change in color, my dying mother resisted the division of cancer cells in her body as they metastasized beyond her lungs to other vital organs and, eventually, to her brain.

A month after she passed, my marriage ended abruptly, and I didn't know which way was up anymore. All I knew was that I wasn't happy. I had worked unimaginably hard in the corporate world for more than a decade, working my way up the corporate ladder, chasing happiness around every bend, but the faster I ran, the further away it was.

As my twenties twilighted, I went searching for answers, looking for anything to help me figure it all out. At that point, any answer would've sufficed.

Then in November 2009, a single tweet changed my life. Someone I followed on Twitter, which I hadn't used much up to that point, shared a link to a video from a young Midwesterner named Colin Wright. Don't ask me why, but for some reason I felt compelled to click the link.

Colin had an interesting story. He too had been

unhappy with the status quo, tired of slaving 70-plus hours a week as a faceless cog in the corporate wheel. But unlike me, Colin had taken action to rid himself of his discontent. He'd quit his job and decided he could work for himself. He decided he could pursue his passions—traveling the world—while making less money. And now he was traveling to a new country every four months based on the votes of his readers.

He said this transition was easy for him because he was a "minimalist."

I didn't have a clue what *minimalism* was, and I certainly didn't have the desire to leave Dayton, Ohio and travel around the world as some sort of peripatetic writer. But remember, I was searching for answers. So when I heard him talk about his newfound freedom, and how minimalism allowed him to focus on the most important things in his life, I immediately said, "I'm in."

I spent the next eight months simplifying my life, shedding the vast majority of my material possessions, though it wasn't always easy; the old saying ends up being true: *the things we own end up owning us*. Over time, we become our things, and our possessions become a part of us —part of our *identity*. But I didn't let that stop me. I knew a more meaningful life was out there, so I kept simplifying, questioning my stuff, forcing myself to give less meaning to my things and much more meaning to my health and my relationships and the most important areas of my life.

By the time the summer of 2010 arrived, I'd drastically simplified the way I live, I'd started paying off my debt, and I was far less reliant on the income that once held me hostage

—an income I'd needed to sustain the ridiculous lifestyle I was leading, a lifestyle that, by the way, had led to much of my discontent.

That summer, I was still working 70 hours a week as the director of operations for 150 retail stores (you can almost taste the irony in that job title, can't you?), but now, with the excess stuff out of my way, I was finding more time to focus on my passion—writing literary fiction. Since I was 22, I'd wanted to write fiction. For me, the made-up world of stories and characters did something magical that no other art form could do: it allowed an exchange of consciousness between the author and his characters and the reader. I was spellbound by this exchange; it created an emotional resonance that made me want to participate, to create, to write. So at 22, I started tinkering around with fiction, writing whenever I could, whenever a free moment presented itself, cobbling together stories of lives far more interesting than the banality of my own corporate-driven existence.

In June 2010, a year before I turned 30, I decided to take a week off work and stay with a friend in Bed-Stuy Brooklyn, a week in which I planned to sort through things and determine the right direction for my life. A day before I left Ohio, I saw another tweet from Colin. He was back in the states for two months, and he wanted to know if anyone had a smartphone he could use.

I did—I had an extra BlackBerry collecting dust in a drawer—so I offered to send it to him. He asked me to mail it to New York City, where he would be for the next week. *Hey*, I thought, *I'll be in New York too. Let's do lunch.*

It just so happened that Colin was starting an indie publishing company, and I wanted some advice about publishing my fiction. I'd been writing for seven years, and I'd become quite good at it, but all I had to show for it was a two-inch-thick stack of rejection letters from scads of literary agents.

In New York, Colin and I ate lunch; he liked my writing, and so he offered me an idea: he said that I should do something online—*anything*—that I should start a website and see what happens. I dismissed this idea at first. Hell, I didn't know how to start a website. And I was completely ignorant to the whole nonfiction genre. So I sat on the idea, not paying it much mind—at first.

Then in October 2010, a year after my mother had died, my best friend, Ryan, began noticing a marked difference in my attitude. For the first time in a long time, I was happy. Life wasn't perfect, and I still wanted to change a shedload, but I was content and it showed. I shared with him what I'd done over the last year to simplify my life, showing him Colin's site, as well as some interesting insights from Leo Babauta, Joshua Becker, Courtney Carver, and Julien Smith (all of whom would eventually become personal friends of mine).

Just as I had a year earlier, Ryan also unearthed the freedom that minimalism brought to his life. Together, we were able to sculpt an interesting (and true!) story from our newfound clutterfree lives. He understood that I was passionate about writing, and I knew he was passionate about helping people change, so I decided to take Colin's initial advice and document our journey online.

The rest of the story is history, as it were, although that history is the most exciting part.

Clueless and fumble-prone, Ryan and I launched a website, *The Minimalists*, on December 14, 2010. And over the next year, something astonishing occurred: people actually found value in our words, and they shared our essays with their friends and loved ones. Our site grew organically and thanks to some incredibly kind people, we were featured all over the web. We left our six-figure corporate jobs and published four books, including my first fiction book, all four of which received phenomenal praise and ended up becoming bestsellers on Amazon. And now, despite the fact that I don't have a college degree, I'm teaching an online writing class to help people who want to learn from my years of writing experience.

Most important, Ryan and I have been able to contribute beyond ourselves. Minimalism has allowed us to shed the excess so we can live intentionally and add value to others. And *that* is the most fulfilling part of this entire journey.

All this, the result of a single tweet. I guess you never know what small decision will lead to great change. I can't imagine what my life would be like if I hadn't leapt down the rabbit hole that day.

Of Course It's Unreasonable, Dummy!

Interview with a Vampire

I recently imagined an elaborate, expansive conversation between my 27-year-old self and my 30-year-old self—myself from yesteryear vs. myself from today. It was not a pretty exchange. Suffice it to say, there was a vast ideological dichotomy between these two guys.

Looking down on their tête-à-tête from some sort of omniscient point of view, this is a small chunklet of what I observed...

My 27-year-old self had it all figured out. He could do no wrong. He was too confident (read: arrogant) for his own good. He had the high-paying job, the fancy title at work, the status of a young corporate executive, the long-term career goals, the short-term spend-more-money-than-I-make goals, the big house, the fancy cars, the big screen TVs, and all the stuff that was eventually going to make him happy once all the puzzle pieces fit together perfectly.

My 30-year-old self had it all figured out, too—but in a radically different way. He knew he had "figured it all out" as soon as he had stopped trying to figure it all out. He knew that he didn't know everything—nor would he ever—but he knew that with every year that passed he would continue to grow.

The slightly older man also found a certain amount of contempt for the younger man, and it was hard for him to hide this disdain. He couldn't believe how his self of yesteryear placed so much importance in his stuff, while he didn't value the most important things in life—things like health, relationships, passions, growth, and contribution.

With that contempt also came pity from the older man —pity for a man who was lost but didn't know he was lost. More than anything, the older man sympathized with the younger man, because he had been on the same path a few years earlier.

The two men talked for a while, stating their points of view. Both men had passionate, seemingly valid arguments and rationalizations for their persuasions. And they each had their incontrovertible dogmas. Or so they thought.

A Glaring Difference

There was one gaping difference between these two men, and you could see it in the younger man's eyes. The 27-year-old man was not happy. Sure, he wore a mantle of happiness and experienced short bursts of pleasure or satisfaction, but he wasn't truly happy, he wasn't happy with his life, he wasn't happy inside. And all the fancy things in the world weren't going to make him content. If anything, those things just upped his requirement for more things to pacify a deeper problem.

These two men talked about happiness. The younger man wasn't sure why he was unhappy. He had everything society told him he was supposed to have—right? The older man suggested that contentment was found within, and that no amount of external factors were going to permute the discontentment within.

The older man attempted to share what he had learned over the last couple years. He shared how he found contentment in his relationships with his close friends, how he found satisfaction in growing as an individual and contributing to other people, how he found happiness in pursuing his passions, not pursuing more stuff.

"So, you just left your high-paying job, got rid of most of your stuff, and started living a *meaningful life*?" the younger man asked in a half-mocking, nihilistic, cynical tone.

"Yes. It didn't happen overnight. It took a couple years of focus. It took a few years of being conscious, a few years of being aware of what's truly important. I had to make a fundamental shift in the way I live my—"

"But most people aren't living that way," the younger man interrupted with a raised voice. He was heated; he felt his way of life—*his entire identity*—was being questioned. After all, he had worked so hard to get all the stuff he had, to get the identity he now possessed. "And who the hell are you to tell me how to live my life?"

"I'm not telling you how to live your life. I'm simply stating the obvious: What you're doing right now is not making you happy. Nor are you on the path to happiness. The path you are on leads to more discontent; I know, because I have been down the same path. Until you focus on what's important—until you focus on what's going on inside you—you won't be happy."

"Whatever! Giving up this lifestyle just to pursue my passions seems incredibly unreasonable," the younger man shouted.

"Of course it's unreasonable, dummy!" The older man snapped back. "Being unhappy and discontent is completely reasonable within our society. We see it every day. Being reasonable means lowering your standards. Being reasonable means doing what everyone else expects you to do. Being reasonable means living an average life. But I'd rather be extraordinarily unreasonable and content and happy. I'd rather live a meaningful, albeit unreasonable, life. Get unreasonable and everything's possible. Forget about being *reasonable*—being reasonable got me into the same pile of shit you're in now."

Changes in the Rearview

Discussing Change

I was talking to a nice guy the other day. He was in dire straits. He laid before me many of his problems. His marriage was crumbling. He was in massive debt. He was making less money than he used to. He was living an unhealthy lifestyle. He was unhappy, depressed, and frustrated with where he was in life. He asked me for my advice. He wanted to know how I changed so many things in my life in such a short period of time.

I explained that I didn't have any advice for him. I told him that he knew his situation better than I ever could, and he likely knew what to do. I asked him what advice he'd give himself if he was in my shoes. He told me what he would say to himself. And, it's funny, all his ideas sounded like great advice.

But he didn't like his own advice because it was too gradual. Plus, his advice wasn't easy. He was recommending small, incremental changes—changes that wouldn't likely make a huge difference right away. Instead, he wanted the magic pill, he wanted something that would radically change his life immediately, he wanted instant gratification. His advice seemed so basic, so intuitive, so vapid that it was obviously not what I did to change my life—obviously I had the secret answer with this whole minimalism thingy.

I said that while I had no advice for him, I could tell him how I changed my life, and he could see if any of those changes were applicable to his situation, and if they were, he could use my life as an example. Then I simply echoed his advice back to him, and applied it to my life. You see, I didn't have a magic strategy either. It took me two long years to get where I am now—one small change at a time.

Two Years of Incremental Changes

Two years ago, I too was unhappy, in debt, out of shape, and stuck.

It took me two years to pay off most of my debt and establish a budget. I focused on paying off one creditor at a time. I allocated every extra dollar to pay off my car. I sold my house and moved into a small apartment. I got rid of any superfluous bills (cable TV, Internet, etc.).

It took me two years to get into the best shape of my life, exercising every day and completely changing my diet over time.

It took me two years to give less meaning to my physical possessions, focusing instead on important relationships, personal growth, and contribution.

It took me two years to get away from corporate America and pursue my passions.

None of it happened overnight. And it certainly wasn't easy, but a lot can change in a year or two. I changed my life by focusing on small changes each day. I focused on those small changes, not on everything I wanted to change. And then, one day, I looked in the rearview mirror and everything was different.

Two Years Later

Author's Note: I wrote this essay exactly one year after leaving my corporate career.

Two Years Ago

My mother died two years ago. Her death was a life-changing, horrific experience for me. But it was also the impetus of every change, big or small, that has occurred in my life over the last two years.

If you would have met me twenty-four months ago and told me how my life was going to change in two years, I would have laughed in your face and called you crazy.

But truth be told, good, bad, or ugly, nearly everything in my life changed in two years, and I'm a different person now because of it—a better person after going through these changes.

Two Years of Change

My mother died on October 8, 2009.

I took my first difficult steps into minimalism by letting go of sentimental items.

I sold my three bedroom suburban house and moved into a smaller apartment in the city (Dayton, Ohio, that is).

I realized that minimalism is not a radical lifestyle, so I fully embraced it.

I took a lot of action to make changes in my life: I got rid of my television. I got rid of the Internet. I got rid of time (no more clocks). I got rid of gifts. I cleared my plate, so I could live in the moment. I donated 90% of my stuff. I stopped upgrading. I started taking my own advice. I began spending time in solitude. I stopped trying to be cool. And I just stopped *trying* all together. I started doing.

I helped my best friend, Ryan, embrace minimalism and live a more meaningful life.

I met and became friends with Colin Wright who was the first person to introduce me to minimalism. He also inspired me to move my writing into the online realm.

I started theminimalists.com with Ryan.

I quit my job.

I got rid of some fairly pernicious relationships that were preventing me from growing.

I strengthened and changed many of my most important relationships and developed some meaningful relationships with new people.

I met some incredibly authentic people who have shaped my life.

I found new ways to add value to people's lives.

I got into the best shape of my life.

A few of my essays and interviews were featured all over the web (including an interview in the *Wall Street Journal*, CBS, NBC, FOX, NPR, and a slew of other places).

I wrote five books, including the best fiction I've ever written.

I turned 30 years old.

I met and became friends with Leo Babauta of Zen Habits who inspired me to live with no goals.

My best friend left the corporate world to help grow our business together.

We grew our website to more than 100,000 monthly readers who spend more than 11,000 hours on our site per month.

Our first book debuted at #4 on Amazon.

My first fiction book reached #1 on Amazon's Bestselling Short Stories list.

And I discovered what it meant to live a meaningful life.

Learning from Mistakes and Bad Choices

I write all the above not to impress you. Rather, I want you to know you can change everything in your life in a year or two.

I've also made a lot of personal mistakes and bad choices, all of which I'm grateful for because they've allowed me to learn more about myself and grow as an individual.

Everything changed for me in two years. It's not easy, but we can accomplish much more than we believe is possible. We can live a meaningful life by taking tiny little actions each day that have a significant long-term impact on our lives.

PART EIGHT

PHILOSOPHY

Security Is a Misnomer

We are but dogs, leashed by fear, thrashing in the collars of our own obligations.

People often hang on to things—jobs, relationships, material possessions—in an effort to feel secure. Unfortunately, many of the things we cling to in search of security, actually drain the satisfaction from our lives, leaving us discontented and overwhelmed.

We hold on to jobs we dislike because we believe there's security in a paycheck. We stay in shitty relationships because we think there's security in not being alone. We hold on to stuff we don't need, just in case we might need it down the road in some nonexistent, more secure future.

But if such accruements are flooding your life with discontent, they are not secure. In fact, the opposite is true. Discontent is uncertainty. And uncertainty is insecurity. Hence, by definition, if you are not happy with your situation, no matter how comfortable it is, then you won't ever feel secure.

Take me, for example. I embraced the ostensible security of my prestigious career and of all the cold trappings of our entropic consumer culture. The super-sized house. The steady paycheck. The pacifying material possessions. I'd purchased all the purchases, accumulated all the accumulations, and achieved all the achievements that were supposed to make me feel secure.

So why didn't I experience real security? Why was I glazed with discontent and stress and depression? Because I had more to lose. I'd constructed well-decorated walls that I was terrified to tear down, becoming a prisoner of my own consumption. My lifestyle, equipped with a laundry list of unquestioned desires, anchored me to my own self-built burdens.

I thought I knew what I wanted, but I didn't know why I wanted it.

It turned out that my steady paycheck made me feel less secure, afraid I'd be deprived of the income I'd grown accustomed to and the lifestyle I'd blindly coveted. And my material possessions exposed countless twinges of insecurity, leaving me frightened that I'd suffer loss of my personal property or that someone would take it from me. So I clutched tighter onto these security blankets.

But you see, it's not the security blanket that ensures a person's security. People latch on to security blankets because there's a deeper fear lingering at the ragged edges of a discontented reality; there's something else we're afraid of. The fear of loss. We're afraid of losing love or respect or comfort.

It's this fear that keeps us tied to mediocrity. We're willing to sacrifice growth and purpose and meaning in our lives, just to hold on to our pacifiers, all the while searching all the wrong places for security, misguidedly programming ourselves to believe there's a strange kind of certainty within uncertainty. But the more we amass—the more we need our stockpile—the more uncertain we feel. Needing more will always lead to a pall of uncertainty and insecurity.

Life isn't meant to be completely safe. Real security, however, is found inside us, in consistent personal growth, not in a reliance on growing external factors. Once we extinguish our outside requirements for the things that won't ever make us truly secure—a fat paycheck, a sybaritic relation, a shiny new widget—we can shepherd our focus toward what's going on inside us, no longer worshiping the things around us.

Sure, we all need a particular level of external security to function: food, water, shelter, clothes, health, personal safety, positive relationships. But if we jettison life's excess, we can find infinite security within ourselves. Security blanket or no, we can be absolutely secure alone in an empty room.

Does Minimalism Make You Complacent?

I was explaining minimalism to a group of people at a dinner one night last month. A guy wearing a post-workday suit-and-tie combo peered at me skeptically when I told him I have no goals, when I told him I have no daily routine, when I told him I have no back-up plan, when I told him I have little concept of time these days, so I often don't know what time of day it is (or even what day of the week it is).

I could tell he was intrigued, but, because he was caught up in his corporate-controlled life, my life seemed incredibly unrealistic to him. That's not entirely his fault—it seemed unrealistic to me two years ago too. Two years ago, my goal-oriented life of "achieving" and working through to-do lists was no different than his.

And then, still in doubt, he posited a question: "If you don't have any goals, then aren't you just being complacent?"

My answer: "Yes, if by *complacent* you mean *content*. You see, minimalism has helped me become content, it has helped me get rid of life's excess and be happy with what I have, it has helped me live a more purpose-driven life. Now, thanks to minimalism, I can focus on what's important, and I don't have to "achieve" to be happy."

Sounds nice, doesn't it? That's because it is.

You too can make the journey. All you have to do is decide that it's right for you and take action.

Shopping or Finding Meaning

Forsake your brothers
Give up on your lovers
To get the things you think you need
— Jay Nash, "Sweet Talking Liar"

Unlike some men, I used to enjoy shopping. The act itself felt therapeutic, and it took my mind off the vapid, empty life I was leading. I bought things to pacify the sadness and discontent within. Clothes, gadgets, and accessories were my holy trinity.

Shackled by the chains of consumerism, I ended up with things I didn't need—things I didn't even *want* much of the time. So I stored those excess things in my basement or my extra closets or in large storage containers stacked in various rooms throughout my oversized house. I didn't use the stuff, but I held on to it just in case.

But I ended up with much more than just the stuff I bought. I ended up with debt from the stuff I financed or purchased with credit cards. And I ended with anxiety from that debt and anxiety from the space the stuff occupied.

Unbeknownst to me, I developed a sense of attachment

to my stuff over time. I didn't question this feeling, I simply accepted it, which made letting go very difficult. All this misguided angst led me to more shopping in an attempt to fill the void I'd created. It was a vicious cycle.

Eventually, when I stumbled across minimalism, my eyes were forced open and I saw a scary new world. I began to realize that this never-ending cycle of consumerism would lead to perpetual discontent—unless I broke the cycle (and only *I* could do it; no one else could do it for me). I realized that while I needed *some* stuff, there was no meaning in my endless consumption loop.

I needed to close the loop.

Not only did I need to stop buying most of the stuff I was buying, but I had to start paring down and getting rid of the stuff I didn't need.

I knew simply getting rid of my stuff wasn't the complete answer. I knew I could get rid of all my stuff and sit in an empty room and be just as miserable as I was before. Rather, I needed to discover what was important in my life; I needed to replace the stuff in my life with meaningful pursuits.

So as I got rid of the excess stuff, I replaced it by focusing on the important aspects of my life: I radically improved my health. I focused on the relationships I had forsaken for so long. I pursued my passion for writing fiction. I found ways to improve daily and grow as an individual. And I began to contribute beyond myself. These are the things that allowed me to do something that shopping could never let me do—they allowed me to live a meaningful life.

Today, less than two years later, a shopping mall feels like an unwelcoming place of chaos, destruction, and anxiety. Today, I'd rather have a memorable experience than negotiate the halls of a crowded shopping mall looking for the crack-cocaine high of yesteryear.

The Rats in the Tunnel

There is a light at the end of the tunnel. Intuitively, we all know this. Even when it's hard to find, we know it's there somewhere—somewhere just beyond the bend, somewhere within reach.

Finding the light isn't the hardest part of life's journey. It's dealing with what's hiding in the tunnel that's incredibly difficult. What lurks in the darkness keeps us from focusing on the light.

Every time I visit New York City, I see oversized rats scurrying down the blackened train tracks below the subway platform. If I were to jump down and walk those tracks, I know I could find the light at the end of the subway tunnel, eventually.

But finding the light isn't what worries me. What worries me are the rats in the tunnel. If I go down there and into the tunnel, I must contend with whatever stalks the darkness waiting to trip me up and keep me from seeing the light.

Metaphorically, the rats are no different than the plethora of pernicious obstacles that get in our way every day—the mundane tasks, the banal distractions, the vapid, harmful ways we pacify ourselves.

Minimalism allowed me to remove those obstacles and focus on the light; it allowed me to shoo the rats from the tunnel and find daylight much quicker. In fact, minimalism allowed me to swiftly get out of the tunnel altogether, eschewing the malevolence of the filthy creatures hiding in the darkness.

And the light is so much brighter when you get out of the tunnel.

What are your rats? What keeps you in the tunnel, hidden from the light? Shopping? Television? Internet? Debt? Clothes? Gadgets and consumer electronics? Overeating? Something else?

What could you get rid of that would allow you to focus on the light? What can you remove from your life to add more meaning?

Minimalism Is Not a Radical Lifestyle

Some people think I live a radical lifestyle when we talk about minimalism. They say things like "I could never be a minimalist."

But the truth is that my lifestyle is not radical. I don't consider myself a radical person. If you met me today and we didn't talk about minimalism (which we probably wouldn't), you wouldn't think my lifestyle is much different from yours:

I don't count my stuff, but I have hundreds of things, even after I got rid of 90% of my stuff. I own a car. I own pots and pans and kitchen utensils. I own a queen-size bed. I own a smartphone. I own a laptop computer. I own a desk. I own a guitar. I own some furniture. I own some books. I own a clothes dresser. I own a washer and dryer. I own more than a few days worth of clothes.

But there are three key distinctions

I don't own excess stuff. I have only the things I use frequently, things that add value to my life; but I don't have extra stuff, I don't have just-in-case items. If I wanted to change my lifestyle, then my definition of "excess" would change as well. For example, if I wanted to become a nomadic writer, traveling the world like my friend Colin Wright, then I'd need to drastically reduce my possessions. (It would be pretty hard to strap that washer and dryer to my back as I traversed the world.) But, at this point in my life, I'm happy with where I live, and I don't desire to travel extensively. If that changes, then I will change.

I constantly question my possessions. Do I still need this? When is the last time I used this? What would happen if I got rid of this? Could someone else use this more than me? These are questions I consistently ask myself. Because I constantly question my possessions, I am in a perpetual state of paring down, which feels good. There is no endgame, I will never *arrive*—I will continue this journey the rest of my life.

I don't give meaning to my possessions. Most important, I understand that my possessions can be replaced. Someone recently asked me what I would grab if my apartment caught fire. "Nothing," I responded. "Everything I own is replaceable."

Minimalism is not a radical lifestyle. It is simply a tool I use to cut the clutter.

How about you—what could you strip away from your life that would allow you to focus on more important aspects of your life?

Is This What You've Been Waiting for Your Entire Life?

A year ago I knew I wasn't happy. I felt the discontent deep inside me. It rattled my bones.

But according to most people—many of the people around me—I had it "figured out." I had the safe, impressive corporate job that nobody questioned and everyone could be proud of. I had the luxury cars, the oversized house, the superfluous stuff that was supposed to make me happy but never did. I also had the debt and the discontent that came with those things. I was a consumer, not a creator.

The worst part was I didn't know how to break the cycle. I was stuck and I didn't know what to do.

I went home one night after a long day at work, loosened my necktie, and contemplated the last thirty years. I literally looked in the mirror and asked the man staring back at me the most important question I've ever asked myself:

Is this what you've been waiting for your entire life?

I knew, at that very moment, that this wasn't what I'd been

waiting for my whole life. I knew that my younger self—although proud of the money and ostensible success of the corporate world—wouldn't approve of what I'd become. And I knew that my future self would look back and wish I'd made a change.

Two days later I sat down with my boss and told him I wanted to move on with my life. I had worked at the same corporation for twelve years, diligently climbing the corporate ladder one rung at time, but it was time for me to move on. We worked out an exit plan together, and in a few months I was out of there without a definitive plan of how to live.

And now, a year later, everything is different. For the first time in my life I can answer that same question much differently: Yes, this *is* what I've been waiting for my entire life.

It's a question worth asking.

Nightmares of a Perfectionist

Perfectionism is a futile endeavor. As a perfectionist, I speak from experience. And this is my confessionary hymn.

At times my perfectionism haunts me. All the pleasure of "getting it right" can be immediately wiped out by small, debilitating imperfections: the sharp stabbing pain of a negative criticism, the disappointment of a brightly-illuminated flaw, the vitriolic feeling brought forth by a set of rolled eyes.

Our culture reinforces certain standards we cannot live up to: the women with their half-a-serving hips adorning the covers of magazines, the expensively-dressed celebutantes wearing an average-person's annual salary on her wrist, the modern rock stars and Fonzarellis plastered all over billboards and TV screens.

Attempting to keep up with these false standards is tantamount to playing a rigged game—the game of Perfectionism is designed for failure. And even if we could win at this game, it wouldn't make us happy. Contentment comes from within, not from the entrapment of protruding hipbones or the bling-bling of consumer purchases. And yet we continue to play this game with religious devotion—myself included.

Airing Out Flaws

Everyone is subject to public scrutiny at some level. Once your thoughts exit your mouth, people will judge you. Once a creation—a new book, a work project, a term paper—is released to the world, even its most subtle flaws are glaring.

But we can't hide every thought, hold back every word, restrain every impulse.

And the fact that we can't mask all our imperfections is actually a good thing. That's because our faults improve us; they help us grow. Once we put our individual problems out in the open, they are far more noticeable, and thus we feel compelled to address those problems.

For example, I've noticed this phenomena within myself and this website. By writing about my life, my transformations, and my continued pursuit of personal refinement, I've "put myself out there," as it were. Many of you know more about me than certain members of my family do. Ergo, my public display of self forces me to grow in ways I wouldn't otherwise grow, allowing me to learn important new lessons about life.

The truth is that we are all human. Thus, we are all imperfect. And if I waited for everything to "be perfect," I'd be waiting in perpetuity, and my writings would never exist. So instead, I write and then release it to the world, warts and all.

Consequently, I've learned a valuable lesson by exposing my blemishes to the world: I've learned to be happy with my efforts and my growth, not with perfection.

Truth be told, I work incredibly hard on everything I do and I'm proud of that fact. It is exciting and gratifying to write these words for you—to create something from nothing. Everything I do is inherently imperfect. And but I'm happy when I can look myself in the mirror and know it's the absolute best I can do.

Similarly, it's just as gratifying to share what I've learned about writing with the students in my online writing class, opening myself up in yet another way, airing out my flaws in front of an intimate audience, finding new ways to learn and prosper.

Irrespective of the arena, whenever I air out my flaws, I grow.

Other Life Examples

I think the same goes for all other areas of life.

Health. If you want a perfect body, you'll never have it. Instead, you can focus on having a *better* body, you can focus on having a *healthier* body while enjoying the process of exercising and strengthening your health.

Relationships. If you're looking for the perfect partner or friend or co-worker, you'll lose every time. People are, by nature, imperfect. We come equipped with a tackle box of flaws. But instead of focusing on the faults, you can focus on making your relationships better and on establishing new, empowering relationships.

Passions. If you're looking for the perfect job, it's not out there. No matter your vocation—even if you land your "dream job" in which you pursue your passions every day—there will be moments of despair, moments of tedium, moments of doubt. But that's OK. Instead of those moments, you can focus on the joy experienced by pursuing your passions, you can focus on the fulfillment you get from improving everything you do in tiny little ways each day.

Every area of life is filled with imperfection, but we needn't neurose over every blemish.

Far from Mediocrity

I am not, however, advocating being *average*. The average person is not happy with his life. I refuse to be run-of-the-mill. I'd rather fail miserably than saunter down the alley of mediocrity. Instead, I'm advocating passionately pursuing what you love and doing so with vigor, knowing that there will be shortcomings and mistakes along the way. I'm advocating learning from those failings—even appreciating them—because they allow you to grow. And that's what life is about.

Taking Feedback for What It Is

And I've learned to take feedback for what it is. Sure, there are some cynics and hypocritical assholes out there, and I've learned to pay them no mind (although that's not always easy). But most people who provide advice are simply attempting to help; they are contributing to the greater good. This feedback allows us to evolve, it allows us to expand and live more meaningful lives.

That doesn't mean that I apply every bit of feedback I receive, but I do consider the meaningful, value-adding observations and take action accordingly.

Dealing with Imperfection by Letting Go of the Negative

I've also learned how to better deal with imperfection. I've learned to do three simple things to change my state when I feel overwhelmed or bothered by my foibles.

Breathe. When Stress knocks on my door, I'll take a walk and focus on my breathing. Deep, diaphragmatic breaths change our physiology, calm us, and provide our bodies with the oxygen we need.

Focus. If we focus on the negative, we'll feel fear, loneliness, jealousy, and every other negative emotion we can conjure from within. Conversely, if we focus on the positive, we'll feel joy, happiness, and contentment. Much of how we feel is directly associated to what we focus on.

Beliefs. Similarly, whatever we believe becomes our reality. If we believe people are rotten and hateful, then we'll find all the flaws in even the nicest people. But if we believe people are kind and caring, then we'll find glimpses of perfection in every miscreant and reprobate. The same is true for any event or situation in which we are involved—it is whatever we believe it is.

Cola and Politics: Follow Your Heart

"There is no such thing as not voting: you either vote by voting, or you vote by staying home and tacitly doubling the value of some Diehard's vote."
—David Foster Wallace

The big presidential election is peeking its gigantic, mass-mediated noggin around the corner. It's almost here, and if we rely solely on the U.S. media for our info, then we might believe we have only two choices: Democrat vs. Republican.

But believing there are only two voting options is like assuming we have only two beverage choices: Coke vs. Pepsi. Clearly, this point of view is flawed. Sure, you might enjoy the taste of one over the other, but they're both essentially the same thing: unhealthy and full of empty calories. That choice is a faux-choice, and is really not a choice at all.

The truth is that we have myriad options, not just Coke or Pepsi, not just Democrat or Republican. We can choose to live more consciously, realizing and understanding our options. Instead of cola, we can drink water or green drinks; instead of the main political parties, we can vote Libertarian or Green Party (or write-in Ryan Nicodemus). Irrespective of our choice, we can ignore what we're "supposed" to do and, instead, follow our hearts.

Aren't we just throwing away our votes then?

If you follow your heart, it's never in vain. Sometimes you have to follow your heart even when you know you're going to lose. That goes for relationships, health, politics, or any other area of life. Because if you follow your heart, you can lose only once. But if you don't, you may lose a thousand times, a trail of scattered regrets strewn throughout the landscape in the rearview.

We have no interest in propagating our own political views here. Rather, we simply want to encourage you to follow your heart. Drink your pop and vote the party line if that's what your heart tells you to do. But if it doesn't, then there are always other options.

Channel Surfing

We're always looking for something better. Something nicer or faster or newer or shinier or bigger. Something more. Something else.

The remote control made this kind of searching easier than ever. You can search a thousand channels without leaving your couch, flipping endlessly through channel after channel after channel until you find something *better*.

But television isn't the only place in which we constantly search for something better. We flip through every aspect of our lives—food, relationships, entertainment, work—all the while looking for something—*anything*—other than what's in front of us.

The problem is that, in a world of unlimited choices, there actually *is* always something better somewhere on another channel. So, even when we find something we like—something we enjoy—it's never enough, and we begin to yearn for something else.

The key, then, is to be happy with the channel you're watching. If you're not happy, take action, change the channel—work hard to change your situation. But once you find something you like, enjoy it. You needn't search in perpetuity.

Once you enjoy your life, you will grow, and eventually the channel will change on its own.

PART NINE

CONSUMER CULTURE

Too Much Branding These Days

There's too much branding going on. I tweeted these six words the other day. I received several questions about this statement, and so I'll attempt to expand on my thoughts here.

First, consider this: there is a difference between a *brand* and *branding*.

McDonald's, Johnson & Johnson, and Walmart are brands. And *you*, if you're a creator of something, can also be a brand. The difference between a *corporation* as a brand and *you* the brand is that the corporation's primary objective is, by definition, to make money. *You*, on the other hand, needn't bear profit as your main objective.

If *you the maker* are concerned principally with earning money by creating something, and yet you pretend this something is being made to benefit the greater good, then your product will reek of insincerity, pretense, and disingenuousness. This is commonplace for corporations, so much so that we've come to expect it in their advertisements —we know that their fundamental goal is money.

For example, have you ever believed that a corporation truly understands *you*? I certainly haven't. Not as an adult at least. But I have regarded as true that certain musicians or authors or artists understand *me* as a person; there is often a connection between me and the artist and her work.

This doesn't mean that products devised for profit aren't useful (they often are); it simply means that people won't find the same connection with that product as they do with literature, music, or artwork they love—for the main objective of these personal works isn't (typically) financial in nature; it is to develop a connection with other human beings.

When making money is the dominant driver for what you create, you are *branding*—carefully composing your image, neurotically considering your demographic, and obsessively tweaking your good or service to fit a customer base.

There's nothing wrong with earning money; I simply prefer for it to result from what I create (not the other way around). I've found that when I'm honest and open and add value to other people's lives, people are willing to support my work whenever they are given the opportunity.

Marketing vs. Advertising

Marketing shouldn't be confused with advertising. Although these two terms are often used synonymously, they shouldn't be.

We're all marketers. Good or bad, we all market ourselves—often unconsciously—and hope that certain people look upon us favorably based on the image we project to the world. There are many fakers, but most individuals are authentic when marketing themselves. That's because most people can detect individual insincerity and reject frauds accordingly.

Advertising is different. The motive behind (most) advertising is primarily financial. Thus, advertising itself is inherently tainted and, in many cases, disingenuous. But ads are everywhere in our heavily-mediated culture, so be careful. Proceed with caution.

Eschewing Advertising in Favor of Authentic Marketing

Modern-day advertisers are nothing but aggregators of eyeballs. They get paid to encourage you to take action. What's the best way to make you act? To highlight your problems of course: to make you think you are inadequate, to showcase your perpetual discontent and then offer a solution from the entrapment of your self-invented restless dissatisfaction.

Just turn on your television, switch on your radio, open your newspapers and magazines, and click the banner ad tailored to your specific needs, tastes, and desires. See, you have scores of problems. You are anxious, tired, stressed, worried, overwhelmed, underpaid, overworked, undervalued, overweight, depressed, too old, too fat, too thin. Your scrawny muscles aren't big enough, your flabby stomach isn't washboard enough, your wrinkled face isn't young enough.

Damn! According to most advertisers, you are a freaking mess.

But fear not, there are myriad solutions tucked into every ad.

Let's face it. We've all been MTV'd and Facebooked. Advertising is everywhere now. The best advertisers and marketers are Mozart-esque in their ability to make you yearn for something you didn't even know existed. But you already have everything you need; you don't have to upgrade. You needn't succumb to cultural norms and societal expectations to allay your fears and pacify your discontentment.

Hell, maybe your life *is* a mess. Even if it is in shambles, as my life once was, no *product* is going to fix your problems. Only you, through deliberate actions over time, can correct yourself. This is not easy—and it certainly is not as sexy as the newest gadget or pill that will solve all your woes—but attempting to fix discontentment with a purchased quick fix is just trying to fix the problem with the problem. Because, truth be told, you can buy all the cure-alls and still not be cured; you can obtain all the shiny new thingamajigs and still not impress anyone.

There will, however, be a new kind of authentic marketing in the future. As we consumers continue to get wiser, as we realize we needn't be fooled by the manufactured unrest promulgated by pop culture, we will begin to find value in genuine people and brands who actually have our best interests in mind.

Thanks to the Internet, this shift has already started. There are brands like Charity Water who actually want to help people. There are individuals who want to add value to people's lives. There are organizations who want to commit to contributing first, not focusing on money as the primary driver for their actions.

Ryan and I, with our writings at *The Minimalists*, do our best to fall into this category. We open our hearts in an effort to help you open your mind. I don't think there's anything wrong with offering products and services, that's how I make a living, but I must add value first if I expect anyone to pay attention in the long run. Maybe that doesn't make me the best advertiser in the world, but it helps me sleep a little better at night. Besides, anything less would be disingenuous.

The Troubling Nature of Pop Culture

We're all slobbering canines, drooling on command for today's Pavlovian advertisements. We grew up with pop drivel invading every dark corner of our media-saturated lives: The glowing box in the living room showcasing *ideal* families in *ideal* homes living *ideal* lives. The car stereo blaring soul-crushing top 40-isms during rush-hour traffic. Newspapers foretelling inescapable doom and irremediable despair without any hope of salvation or redemption. Magazines twaddling the latest gossip about *such and such* and *what's his name.*

Our collective brains have soaked up the meaningless muck and are now waterlogged with platitudes and cultural niceties and the false expectations of the way life should be.

Snap! Crackle! Pop!

American Express: Never leave home without it. Coca-Cola: It's the real thing. McDonald's: I'm lovin' it.

We know these corporate slogans—and many others—by heart. We've let them in without even knowing we were letting them in. And but by now we've accepted these mantras as maxims by which we should make our decisions.

If someone continuously repeats a lie, does it eventually

become the truth? Is it not safe to leave our homes without our credit cards? Is the realest thing in our lives an aluminum can of carbonated sugarwater? Do we really *Love* the golden arches?

Even Pringles admits that they know we are programmed: *Once you pop, you can't stop!* Sadly, they're right. It's incredibly difficult to shake the sedative weight of everything we've learned from pop culture. But fortunately, once you go pop, you *can* stop. Although it isn't easy.

Ain't Nothin' on the News but the Blues

We never opted-in to pop culture. It already had us in its sinister clutch at birth, an invisible umbilical cord that no one ever thought to cut.

After all, what's the harm in a little TV, in a little late-night news, in catching up on the day's current events? In reality, there's nothing wrong. But when we simply accept the idiot box's catchy one-liners as epigrams by which we must make our most important decisions, then we get lost rather quickly.

It's easy to be passively entertained and informed, accepting catchphrases to be self-evident. Even the news these days has to be "info-tainment" so that it's more palatable to the casual listener (read: consumer).

That's because it's easy to be entertained, but it's hard work to seek out the truth, it's difficult to form our own opinions based on multiple points of view, and it's much easier to allow someone else—be it Rush Limbaugh or Keith Olberman or a faceless corporation with a seemingly endless marketing budget—to form an opinion for us.

Besides the issue of its inherently passive nature, today's commercial-riddled pop-information can't inform us of life's larger problems, of our deepest troubles and fears, of what it actually means to be alive—what it means to be a human being in the most complex time in human history.

Suffice it to say, the American Dream is broken. It has been for decades. And attempting to go back to "the way things were" will not fix it. "Fixing it" would only perpetuate the inevitable, making it worse in the long-run. The longer we put off our troubles, the harder they are to deal with.

Instead, as a culture, *we* must take responsibility. We must fix ourselves. We must create the disciplines necessary to be alive in this complex world. We must become *aware* of what's going on around us so that ultimately we can be aware of what's going on *inside* us. Only then will we be able to know what's truly important.

Considering the Audience

"I don't have an audience; I have a set of standards."
—Don DeLillo, Paris Review 1992

Do you consider your audience when you're writing?

I often get a variation of this question from readers and from students in my writing class, and the answer is not as simple one might think. My first inclination is to say, "No." But that's not entirely true. If I'm being honest with myself, then ultimately the answer is yes *and* no.

No in the sense that I am not a demographer. I don't sit down and attempt to craft a message for 35–55-year-old white females or high school sophomores with divorced parents (though both demographics read my essays). Nor do I sit down and attempt to write something that will appeal to the largest possible audience. Doing so would result in a shittily crafted product. Constantly worrying about what others *might* think, a) is a futile endeavor, and b) can be disingenuous. This is, in fact, why we removed comments from our website—because we didn't want to cater our message to the 0.1% of naysayers stalking the comment threads.

But the answer is *yes* in the sense that when I do consider the reader, he or she looks rather suspiciously like me. Not that he's (or she's) a 31-year-old, 6'2", white male from the Midwest, but I assume that my audience thinks much like I do. That is, my typical reader is open minded, inquisitive, introspective, and struggles with important life issues, just like me. My typical reader is inherently flawed, just like me. This is where we make a connection.

Thus, I don't attempt to craft a message that will appeal to everyone; I simply write for you—someone who thinks much like I do. We will disagree from time to time—even I disagree with myself at times—but we're both receptive to new ideas and we're willing to change our minds.

There are obvious examples in which this form of creating would not work—the Jitterbug cellphone, children's diapers, many medications—but for many creative types, it seems best to consider yourself as the audience. Because with all our differences, there are millions of people just like me and you.

PART TEN

WORK

Work-Life Balance
An Unpublished Essay

I used to think of *work* as a bad word. During my dozen years in the corporate world, *work* was something that prevented me from living, something that kept me from feeling satisfied or fulfilled or passionate, and thus the word itself carried with it a negative connotation.

When I left the corporate world to pursue my dream, I swore off the word for a long time. Noun, verb, or adjective, I avoided all of *work*'s iterations.

I no longer "went to work," so that was easy to remove from my lexicon. I no longer "worked," instead I replaced the word with a more specific verb. I would "write" or "teach" or "speak" or "volunteer," but I refused to "work." I no longer went to the gym to "workout," opting instead to "exercise." I stopped wearing "work clothes," choosing instead to wear "dress clothes." I avoided getting "worked up," preferring to call it "stress" or "anxiety." I didn't bring my car to the shop to get "worked on," deciding instead to have my vehicle "repaired." I even avoided "handiwork" and "housework," selecting their more banal alternatives. Suffice it to say, I wanted nothing to do with the word. I wanted it stricken from my memory, erasing every shred of the thing that kept me from pursuing my dream for over a decade.

But after a year of this nonsense, I realized something: it wasn't the word that was bad; it was the meaning I gave to the word. It likely took a year of removing the word from my everyday speech to discover that it wasn't a bad word at all. During that year, I had been pursuing my dream, and guess what, when I looked over my shoulder at everything I had accomplished, I realized that pursuing my dream was, in fact, a lot of work. It took a lot of work to grow a website. It took a lot of work to publish five books. It took a lot of work to embark on a 33-city coast-to-coast tour. It took a lot of work to teach my first writing class. It took a lot of work to pursue my dream.

Work wasn't the problem. What I did as my work was the problem. I wasn't passionate about my work before—my work wasn't my mission—and so I wanted to escape from work so I could live a more rewarding life, looking to balance out the tedium of the daily grind.

But work and life don't work that way. Even when you're pursuing your dream, there will be times of boredom and stress and long stretches of drudgery. That's alright. It's all worth it in the end. When your work becomes your life's mission, you no longer need a work-life balance.

The High Price of Pursuing My Dream

It turns out that the American Dream was never *my* dream. Rather, it was competing with my dream, clouding over my revelatory desire to be a literary writer. The big house, the fancy car, the impressive job title, the six-figure salary, the superfluous stuff. I had all of it. But none of it made me happy. And none of it allowed me to pursue my dream.

Instead, there was a void. Something was missing. I didn't know what that void was, and working 70–80 hours a week didn't give me much time to explore its cavernous interior.

And so before I left my job last year, I had to pay the price for my self-indulgent twenties as that scarred decade descended into the cloud-cluttered horizon. I could no longer afford the lifestyle I'd been living during my mindless twenties, a cog in a wheel of greed and lust and happenstance. Instead, it was far more important for me to pursue my dream—to pursue my passion for writing—than it was for me to keep living that empty, opulent lifestyle, a lifestyle which, by the way, was *not* bringing me happiness.

Thus, pursuing my dream didn't come without a cost. Before I left my career to become a full-time writer, I spent two years paying off the vast majority of my debt: credit card debt, student loans, medical bills, and the like. Then I paid off my car and sold my large house and eventually moved into a small, $500-per-month apartment.

Then, over time, I gradually got rid of nearly all my bills, committing to less commitments.

I no longer have the Internet at home. Instead, I now find more productive things to do with my time, focusing on my health and my relationships and the more important things in life. When I need to use the Internet, I go to the library or a coffee shop and I use it deliberately, no longer wasting hours of my life "surfing the web." Living my dream doesn't allow time for such pillory.

No more TV. Instead, I read or write or go to a concert or a movie with a friend, creating meaningful, lasting experiences instead of channel surfing my life away. Living my dream doesn't allow time for such passive nonsense.

No more expensive gym membership. Now, I walk more than ever, and I exercise each day at home or in the park. And at age 31, I'm in the best shape of my life.

No more extra bills. No new expensive cars. No more satellite radio. No more expensive cellphone plan. No more Netflix. No more magazine subscriptions. Hell, I even stopped buying material possessions for a year. Living my dream makes these ephemeral pleasures pale in comparison.

And now my only bills at this point are rent, utilities, and insurance. Everything else had to go. I decided that pursuing my dream was worth it.

I now make less money than I did a decade ago. But I've never been happier.

That happiness didn't come without a price, though. It

meant getting uncomfortable, questioning my stuff, and getting rid of my crap. It meant refocusing my finances and re-prioritizing my life. It meant living more deliberately and intentionally. It meant I had to stop living the lie and start living my dream, moving forward with a new life of focus and passion and purpose—and far less stuff.

Since then, I've written the best literature of my life, and I've never felt more alive.

How about you: is your dream worth the sacrifices you need to make?

Life's Most Dangerous Question

What do you do? This is often the first question we ask strangers. On the surface, it seems like an ordinary question, one we ask each other every day, a servile four-word nicety we utter so we have something—*anything!*—to talk about.

Let's face it, the majority of the answers are boring, soundbite-ish ripostes we have standing by at the ready, prepped for the next dinner party or networking event: *I am a director of operations. I am a regional manager. I am the senior vice president of who gives a shit.*

Whoopee-do. Good for you.

Truth be told, we regurgitate these canned answers because they're easy to repeat, trance-like and semi-conscious, over and over and over again. No one wants to talk about their boring day job ad nauseam, but it sure is easy to state your name, rank, and serial number; it's easy to prove that you're a cog in the wheel or a rung on the ladder —just like everyone else. It's much harder, however, to talk about other, more important aspects of life. So, instead of finding more meaningful discussions, we go about our days providing lifeless answers to this lifeless question, our collective discs set to repeat.

But let's think about this question for a moment. In

reality, it's such a broad, salient inquiry that any answer would suffice. What do I do? I do a lot of things: I drink water. I eat food. I write words on little yellow legal pads.

Once you scrape away its cheap gold-plating, however, you'll find a series of pernicious inquisitions lurking beneath the surface. Sadly, what we're actually asking when we posit this malefic question, albeit unknowingly, is:

How do you earn a paycheck? How much money do you make? What is your socioeconomic status? And based on that status, where do I fall on the socioeconomic ladder compared to you? Am I a rung above you? Below you? How should I judge you? Are you worth my time?

There is a better way to answer this dangerous query, though: by changing the question altogether.

The next time someone asks you what you do, try this: Don't give them your job title. Instead, tell them what you're passionate about, and then change course by asking them what they are passionate about:

"What do you do?" asks the stranger.

"I'm passionate about writing (or rock climbing or sailing or input accounting)," you say, followed by, "What are you passionate about?"

At this point, you'll likely get one of three responses: 1) a blank stare, 2) the person will tell you that they're also passionate about X, Y, or Z, and the conversation will veer off in a more meaningful direction, or 3) the stranger will attempt to recite their job title, to which you can respond, "That's great. So you're passionate about your job?"

Eventually, you will both be able to discuss the things you enjoy, instead of the job you don't.

I practiced this exercise during my last year in the corporate world. It helped me remove the importance of my job title from my life and ultimately opened me up to discussing my passion for writing with others. Sure, I had an impressive job title, but it didn't make me happy; it didn't fulfill me. And now I'm more fulfilled by my passions than by any title.

Think of this shift as *changing a noun into a verb*. Instead of giving people a title (i.e., a box to put you in), let them know what you enjoy doing—what you're passionate about—and then discover what they enjoy, as well. The conversation will morph into something far more interesting, and you'll learn a lot more about each other than your silly little job titles.

Create Your Masterpiece, a 16-Step Guide

Do you wish you could create something meaningful? Do you wish you had the time to work on that thing you've always wanted to produce—that novel, that piece of art, that passion project?

No need to keep wishing your life away. Based on my experience—i.e., years of procrastination, followed by a couple years of rigorous work, resulting in two personal masterpieces—I've written a 16-step guide to get you started on your own masterpiece.

If I could fire up the Delorean and rewind the last decade, this is everything I would tell my 21-year-old self about creating meaningful work. It would have been harsh, but I needed it, and it would have saved me a ton of heartache. Feel free to listen in.

Step 1. Look yourself in the mirror. It's time for you to be honest with yourself, young Josh. Either you're accomplishing what you want to accomplish or you're not. There is no in-between. If it's the latter, then you must admit to yourself that you are the only person preventing you from pursuing your passion project. Denial is a heartless bitch; so the first step is looking in the mirror and admitting that you haven't even scratched the surface on creating something meaningful.

Step 2. Kill your distractions. Make a list of everything getting in your way. Surfing the 'net too much? Get rid of the Internet at home. Are certain people draining all your time? Get rid of your shitty relationships. Are material possessions getting in the way? Get rid of your crap.

Step 3. Make time every day. None of us were born equal. We come from different backgrounds, different cultures, different socioeconomic situations. Suffice it to say, we were not all born on a level playing field. Time is the one exception. The only thing we all have in common is time. We all have the same 24 hours in a day. So, get up at 3:30 a.m. if you have to. Find 30 minutes before you leave for work. Work through your lunch break. Find an hour after work. If you want it bad enough, you'll find the time. You have the same amount of time as everyone else who has ever created a masterpiece.

Step 4. Stop making excuses. *I should do this. I should do that. I should, I should, I should.* Too often, we should all over ourselves. You must instead make change a must. *I must create a masterpiece! I must make time every day! I must kill my distractions!* Those musts sound far more empowering than your shoulds, don't they?

Step 5. Stop worrying. Most people are going to praise you for what you do—they'll be proud of your masterpiece once it's finished—but instead we tend to worry about the naysayers. Guess what: people are going to judge you. Some people are going to think what you're doing is stupid. Others will think you've lost your mind. But what other people think doesn't matter. They will be dead soon. And so will you and I. So we better get to work.

Step 6. Grow a pair of balls.

Step 7. Take incremental action. Nearly all masterpieces share two commonalities: time and action. Said another way, you have to do the work every day. You won't create your masterpiece overnight, so don't try. It's far more important to work on it each day. In the course of time, your daily actions will add up immensely. Eventually, you'll look in life's rearview mirror and everything will be different.

Step 8. Change your physiology. Your brain and your body aren't standing in opposite corners of the room. If you want to stimulate your mind, you must stimulate your body. So do something physical. Anything: Walk. Run. Hit the gym. Try yoga. Breathe. Exercise for 18 minutes a day. Trek 500 miles. Just do something to get your body moving. Motion creates emotion.

Step 9. Focus. Focus on your masterpiece. Whatever you focus on, you'll create. Think your project is crappy? Then it will be crappy. Think you'll get it done no matter the odds? Then you'll finish it even if you get hit by a bus.

Step 10. Change your beliefs. One of the biggest reasons we don't accomplish what we set out to accomplish is our limiting beliefs. For years you've told yourself that you'll never be this, you'll never do that, you'll never be good enough. But you're no different than the people who have constructed their masterpieces. The people who create something special—something lasting—aren't necessarily smarter or funnier or better or more toothsome than you. They simply believed they could do it, and through this belief they didn't let anything stand in their way.

Step 11. Become obsessed. Half of passion is love; the other half, obsession. Your masterpiece will feed off your obsession, growing mightily the more obsessed you become. Eventually, you'll wake up thinking about it. You'll go to bed thinking about it. You'll think about it in the bathroom stall. This is good. Let your masterpiece become your obsession. Let it take over.

Step 12. Cut the fat. Brevity is the soul of wit. Or perhaps, more accurately, brevity is wit. My friend Julien Smith's book, *The Flinch*, is intentionally brief. The entire thing can be tweeted, page by page, line by line. Every line was carefully considered. Same goes for *Days After the Crash*—a year of work, boiled down to less than 50 pages. Sure, a masterpiece can be longer and more oblique and digressive —but does it need to be? Realize that you too can build something massive and then chisel it down to its essence. Do this and people will find value in your work.

Step 13. Get the old guard out of the way. Are gatekeepers getting in your way? Can't talk to the person you want to pitch? Can't find an agent or a publisher willing to give you the time of day? Can't get on CNN or MTV? So what! Do it yourself. For the first time in history, you don't need the old guard. We live in an era where the Indians can circumvent the chiefs, taking their masterpieces straight to the tribe.

Step 14. Make it inexpensive. Money was never the goal of your masterpiece, was it? No. You wanted people to hear your album or read your book or view your art—to see, hear, feel, smell, and taste your masterpiece. So remove your boundaries and make it cheap (or give it away). Let it go. It's no longer yours anyway—it belongs to the world.

Step 15. Breathe. Pause and bask in the glory of your masterpiece. Go ahead: take it all in. Enjoy the moment. You deserve it.

Step 16. Do it again. Return to step one. Get started on your next masterpiece. This lifetime can contain as many masterpieces as you allow. Lather, rinse, repeat.

This essay was inspired by the "homework assignment" my friend Julien Smith asked me to write for his website, InOverYourHead.net. You can pick up Julien's masterpiece, The Flinch, for free at Amazon. Both of my masterpieces, Falling While Sitting Down *and* Days After the Crash, *are available inexpensively on Kindle and in print.*

Woodshedding & the Pseudo-Thoreau Thing

Sometimes a man has to go away to come back.

Accordingly, I'm moving to Montana. No, that is *not* a typo. As of October 1, 2012, Ryan and I are residents of the Treasure State, two Ohio transplants residing in a remote cabin about an hour outside Missoula, two hours from the Idaho panhandle, sort of doing an updated version of the whole Thoreau thing (with Wi-Fi).

It's every author's clichéd dream—to find a mountainside cabin with picturesque views, to toss another log on the crackling winter fire as snow blankets the ice-covered river beyond the windowpanes, to remove the distractions of the emotionally exhaustive rat race and start working on his or her most important work—right?

Alright, maybe that's not everyone's aspiration, but after last week's publication of our new book, *Simplicity: Essays*, and after *The Minimalists*' beautiful website redesign by our friends at Spyr Media, the time seemed right for Ryan and I to do just that: to relocate to a secluded spot in Big Sky Country to work vigorously, learn ferociously, and grow immensely.

Consequently, for the next three months, we are going to hole up in our new home in the wilderness and *focus*.

Why Montana?

You might be asking yourself: This guy could live anywhere in the world; why'd he choose Montana as his new home?

Good question. To tell the truth, I wouldn't've even considered Montana until Ryan and I finished our 33-city meetup tour, during which tour we witnessed an entire spectrum of beautiful places throughout the United States and Canada; we visited 40 states and innumerable big cities and small towns, and we discovered much of North America's greatest offerings, from the bright lights and bustling streets of Chicago and NYC to the sunset beaches of San Diego and St. Petersburg, FL.

And so when the tour was over, we shuttled our tour bus (Ryan's little 2004 Corolla) from Vancouver to Ohio, and we traveled through the most beautiful place we'd ever caught sight of: Western Montana, driving past its buffalo-plaid plains and evergreen mountains and skylines from a cowboy cliché, and past its cobalt rivers overhung with century-old pines with flecklets of sunlight through them on the water bending downriver, to the place beyond its sprawling canyons, where fields divided by train cars simmer in the summer heat and time stands still.

I knew it then: she was the one. Montana, rightfully christened The Last Best Place, was the place I wanted to go to finish the work I'd started and begin working on our next big thing(s). The time had come for Ryan and I to hunker down and do some serious work, what musicians often refer to as *woodshedding.*

Woodshedding: Doing the Work and Enjoying It

To get what you want, you must be willing to take action; you must be willing to do the work.

These days, I have little desire for new material possessions (although that baleful yearning still lingers from time to time), but I do want to be successful. And success for me has little to do with money or possessions or status. Rather, success is a simple equation: Happiness + Growth + Contribution = Success. That's the only kind of success I know. Hence, I want to partake in work that makes me happy, work that encourages me to grow, work that helps me contribute beyond myself. Ultimately, I want to create more and consume less. Doing so requires real work.

When I left the corporate world last year, "work" was a dirty word; it held a negative connotation. But now that I'm passionate about the work, I want to do it because I know it helps me grow and it adds value to people's lives. And that means I have a lot of work to do in the coming months…

Finishing the Year the Right Way

Primarily, I'm headed westward to work on my next big thing: a new narrative nonfiction project tentatively titled *Struggles*.

Struggles is my experiment at marrying several genres of writing by blurring the lines between memoir, narrative nonfiction, morally instructive prescriptive nonfiction, fictive story-telling, creative nonfiction, literature, fractured narrative, blogging, and audio recording.

Because it's a work in progress, I'll omit most of the

details other than to say that this project will focus on my story—highlighting my deep personal struggles, past and present—in ways I haven't yet been able to discuss.

Additionally...

Before the sun sets on 2012, I'm going to publish two more (already written) books: my solo essay collection, *A Day in the Life of a Minimalist* (i.e., the book you're reading right now), and my novel, *As a Decade Fades*, which novel took nearly four years to write. I will also publish audiobook versions of these books, as well as audiobooks for several of our existing books.

Ryan will continue to write his current book-in-progress, *Unstuck*, a book designed to show people how to identify the obstacles in their lives and develop a specific plan to remove those obstacles—going from stuck to unstuck.

Furthermore, I'll don my professorial cap and teach the fall semester of my sold-out online writing class, *How to Write Better*, as well as a fiction/narrative nonfiction class in January. And Ryan will continue to take on five new private mentoring clients each month.

What's more, Ryan and I will embark on another, albeit smaller, book tour to coincide with a few upcoming national media appearances and speaking engagements we have planned in the coming months.

Lastly, we recently inked publishing contracts between our publishing company, Asymmetrical Press, and three talented authors: Shawn Mihalik, Chase Night, and Robyn Devine. These are the first three people to sign with

Asymmetrical. All three authors will publish books through Asymmetrical in 2013.

And of course, we'll continue to publish free, quality content regularly on our website. The essays at *The Minimalists* remain our top priority.

Although my plate appears full, it's not because I piled on a bunch of work at once. That would be silly. In fact, I did the opposite. The above productivity-stack is the culmination of several years of hard and steady—yet enjoyable—work. I took on new projects one at a time, only when I felt comfortable with where I stood, only when I knew I could handle them, only when I was certain I could produce high-quality content. Now that it's all coming to a head, I need to focus.

Here's how I plan to stay focused in our little cabin in MT:

How I'll Stay Focused

Habits. Routines breed habits. While bad routines breed bad habits, the opposite is also true. By shedding many of the distractions in my life, I'll become even more focused on what's important, developing the muscle of good habits—diet, exercise, relationships, meditation, contemplation, consistently doing the work, &c.—allowing me to be more productive in an attenuated timeframe.

Variety. I've lived in Ohio my entire life, and during my travels over the last year, I've learned that variety sparks creativity, inspiration, excitement, and lasting contentment.

Variety also means dealing with uncertainty. There is a direct relationship between someone's ability to handle uncertainty and his or her happiness.

Impermanence. On a long enough timeline, everything is ephemeral. Whether it's a 30-year mortgage or a month-to-month lease, nothing lasts forever. I want to embrace this impermanence and enjoy the moment, enjoy my habits, enjoy the work, and enjoy my life. I want to enjoy the good times and then let them go; I want to learn from my mistakes and failures and then let those go, too.

Active vs. passive engagement. I'm not a robot, so of course I'll still have downtime. But I want to use that time mindfully, which means involving myself in active activities vs. passive ones. Instead of veg-out in front of the television, I will opt to wake early and read or meditate or hike or hit the slopes at the nearby ski resort (whose slopes happen to be viewable from our new home's window). I'm also going to try my hand at writing music, a fun endeavor that'll help me grow (Ryan is a closet crooner, while I for the longest time have been a wannabe songwriter).

What's Next?

Are you moving back to Ohio after your stint in Montana? The honest answer is that I don't know where I'll end up after this; I don't have any specific plans. I love Dayton; there are many people I love there; it's a great city—blue collar and unpretentious and small enough to not get lost in the rapacious lights of a big city—and thus I might soon move back to the birthplace of aviation. Or I might stay in Montana. *Or* I might go somewhere completely different. But I'm here now; I'll embrace this impermanence and see what happens around the bend.

One thing's for sure, though: whatever is "next" for *The Minimalists*, it must allow me to grow as an individual; it must allow me to contribute to others in meaningful ways. Ergo, the possibilities are endless.

JOSHUA FIELDS MILLBURN left his corporate career at age 30 to become a full-time author and writing instructor. His essays at *TheMinimalists.com* have garnered an audience of more than 100,000 monthly readers. Millburn is the bestselling author of three fiction and four nonfiction books and has been featured on *CBS This Morning*, ABC, NBC, FOX, NPR, CBC Radio, *Wall Street Journal*, *USA Today*, *New York Times*, *Forbes*, *Boston Globe*, *San Francisco Chronicle*, *San Francisco Examiner*, *Chicago Tribune*, *Chicago Sun-Times*, *Seattle Times*, *Toronto Star*, *Globe & Mail*, *Vancouver Sun*, *Village Voice*, *LA Weekly*, *Zen Habits*, and various other outlets. He was born in 1981 and currently lives in Montana by way of Dayton, Ohio. Read more at his website, JoshuaFieldsMillburn.com.

BOOKS BY JOSHUA FIELDS MILLBURN

FICTION
Falling While Sitting Down: Stories
Days After the Crash: A Novella
As a Decade Fades: A Novel

NONFICTION
Minimalism: Essential Essays
Minimalism: Live a Meaningful Life
A Day in the Life of a Minimalist
Simplicity: Essays
Everything That Remains

MORE INFO
JoshuaFieldsMillburn.com
TheMinimalists.com
Twitter: @JFM

ACKNOWLEDGEMENTS

SPECIAL THANKS TO Leo Babauta, Julien Smith, Joshua Becker, Courtney Caver, and, of course, Colin Wright for inspiring me to take this journey; it's been a hell of a ride and I appreciate your initial push and continued friendship. Big thanks to Ryan Nicodemus for his friendship and for enduring this journey with me; we'll always be brothers. Thank you to my closest friends and loved ones for your ongoing support. Thank you to the people who helped make this collection appreciably better with their editing and proofreading efforts: Aline Reynders, Jodi Dean, Brian Dyer, Sherwynne Pineda Hughes, Rachel Adams, Nina Kovner, Donald Norman, Ashley Maden, and Jen Burkhardt. And thank you everyone who reads my words. I appreciate you.

JFM

CPSIA information can be obtained at www.ICGtesting.com
Printed in the USA
BVOW04s2155050214

344115BV00001B/5/P